DR KIERAN MERVYN AND ROHAN JOHNSON

Overcoming and Becoming

The Art of Managing Change

Best Wishes!

Finncara

First edition

ISBN: 978-1-80-049151-9

Cover art by Divine Orji

This book was professionally typeset on Reedsy.
Find out more at reedsy.com

TO THOSE WHO OVERCAME AND LEAD BY EXAMPLE

Contents

Preface

"Overcoming and Becoming" beckons you to explore a path of healing and renewal. In its pages, you will discover not only each author's personal authentic quests but also a reflection of the potential within each of us. It is an honour to bear witness to this extraordinary story, and I wholeheartedly endorse this powerful testament to our inner resilience and strength."

  -Jonathan Bossaer

We have all had those "life-changing" moments, experiences, or challenges, some more intense than others and some that others could not imagine enduring, let alone surviving. The Cambridge Dictionary defines surviving as "continuing to live or exist". In contrast, the Oxford Dictionary offers more precision of "to continue to live or exist despite a dangerous event or time".

Life's adversities continue and become more challenging as you lose jobs or are overlooked for that well-deserved promotion because you don't get involved in office politics or part-take in any form of shenanigans. To conquer your fears, self-doubt, insecurities, or lack of confidence, you must first examine the underlying causes, whether they stem from a change in personal circumstances, past experiences, social pressures, or a natural susceptibility to being insecure or prone to suffer from anxiety.

In this book, the authors have demonstrated that surviving adversity is much more than surviving "the adversity". They endeavour to show you that surviving "adversity, change, trauma, or setbacks" is to wipe the slate clean, make a fresh start, get out of the rut, and move on from the adverse, traumatic, or life-changing situation.

Ironically, for the most part, it appears easier to wallow in self-pity, hold on to being the victim, and succumb to people's expectations of how you will 'be' in continuing with the pattern of whichever challenging circumstance you may encounter. However, you could try to reinvent yourself, learn to cope and function effectively to heal and fit into a society that can consist of a lot more aggressive and intense behaviour than any dysfunctional home or personal distressing experience.

"The more resilient you are, the better you're able to tolerate the feelings of stress, anxiety, and sadness that accompany trauma and adversity—and find a way to rebound from setbacks."

Resilience reflects your passion to achieve and your capacity to overcome the inevitable challenges or life-changing circumstances you must encounter as you strive to create your desired future. Indeed, you can tap into the reservoir of "inner hope", the self-drive, the fragment of being worthy to overcome and achieve despite the odds being stacked against you, inspiring others to model your behaviour. Works of literature identify 'resilience' as a critical trait for those surviving adversity. Yet, 'perseverance' and 'self-determination' would appear to merit equal credit for those learning to live in a world that presents less obvious challenges than the adversities alone.

Epictetus, a revered Greek Stoic philosopher who lived a simple, minimalistic life, opines that "circumstances don't make the man; they only reveal him to himself." Epictetus was a man who was thought to have been born into slavery. Yet, it hardly needs to be said that his legacy of great inspirational and life-changing quotes positively inspired and transformed the lives of many over the past centuries.

In the same vein, another great iconic and inspirational figure worth mentioning is Nelson Mandela, a well-respected anti-apartheid activist and late president of South Africa, who wrote in his letter to Winnie Mandela, "Difficulties break some men but make others. No axe is sharp enough to cut the soul of a sinner who keeps trying, one armed with the hope that he will rise even in the end."

Building a life in this fast-paced world laced with volatility and uncertainty can be hard for you to endure, and one that certainly takes energy that you may find has already been depleted. However, "hope" drives us, albeit that hope is fragile. It is built on nothing but inner fragments of self-belief.

In Mandela's *Long Walk to Freedom* autobiography, on life's obstacles, he wrote, "I have discovered the secret that after climbing a great hill, one only finds that there are many more hills to climb. I have taken a moment here to rest, to steal a view of the glorious vista that surrounds me, to look back on the distance I have come. But I can rest only for a moment, for with freedom come responsibilities, and I dare not linger, for my long walk is not yet ended."

In his letter to cricketer Makhaya Ntini, he said, "Everyone can rise above their circumstances and achieve success if they are dedicated to and passionate about what they do." His view and purpose in living a meaningful life far exceeds a life lived by a commoner. In his own words, he believes that "What counts in life is not the mere fact that we have lived. It is what difference we have made to the lives of others that will determine the significance of the life we lead."

True leaders rely on experiential learning for self-development and growth to overcome challenges; they are your common man simply trying to learn and craft a new skill, drawing from previous experiences and knowledge intrinsically rooted in life's purposes.

To survive intense adversity, your goal is to become victorious and rise above those old disparaging thoughts that could become your self-made shackles or obstacles, impeding your dreams, aspirations, ambitions, and future prosperity.

Surviving a range of intense and continual disappointments while trying to live up to societal expectations is one of the most complex challenges. Surviving adversity requires resilience and determination to manage "setbacks" from an intensely judging society, whether interpreting low grades as a failure – rather than success for having continued and tried that one might live life to the fullest.

But the truth is, our attitudes, actions, and choices often might inhibit us from reaching our full potential. You see, our state of mind and behaviour sometimes act like obstacles blocking our successes. However, we might not even be aware of the challenges as they are usually firmly entrenched in our thought patterns, masquerading as everyday choices, and so having a persistent crippling influence over our lives to create the future we had envisioned.

Be mindful that creating and fostering a highly fulfilling, rewarding personal and professional life is imperative to survive adversity; nonetheless, it necessitates self-determination and a resilient attitude toward life. Whether you are a survivor or not, be kind, be patient, and do not expect to be told the specific details. Ultimately, overcoming and becoming emotionally, personally, or professionally resilient is challenging yet rewarding. Every hardship faced is an opportunity for growth, and every success is a testament to resilience, self-development, and perseverance.

In this book, "Overcoming And Becoming," the authors guide you (the reader) on overcoming adversities, adapting to change, and becoming the best version of yourself. Organised into thirteen chapters, this book embodies the authors' journey as they share their experiences, which, interestingly, became an integral part of their developmental growth, helping them to become highly successful achievers. Besides, this book presents a comprehensive list of heartfelt, deeply thoughtful, real-life transformational stories that provide practical tips, strategies, and expert advice to help anyone or even you improve your physical and psychological well-being, understand your emotions, nourish your mental health, and cultivate mindful living.

The story starts with "transforming obstacles into stepping stones", as the authors delve into the process of overcoming obstacles and becoming the leader you are meant to be by embracing change, learning from your experiences, rising to the challenge, and making a lasting impact in your personal and professional life.

Fundamentally, this book embodies the authors' journeys and represents the degree of challenges and adversities they have endured at some point in life but still managed to generate insights and value from significant challenges.

Yes, it's true, it's not easy. Life is hard. But we pray that after reading this beautiful piece, you will be empowered to discover your true power and make meaningful changes. We suggest living a life of contentment, freedom, and happiness by taking responsibility and making your luck. If you're looking for something meaningful beyond the usual leadership books, check out this list of chapters in this self-help book that can help you become the best version of yourself.

by Prof. Juanita Illingworth & Rohan Johnson

Acknowledgement

"Overcoming And Becoming" has been a significant and personal undertaking, accomplished through the efforts of some extraordinary and resilient individuals.

You may find that some of their experiences are not gratifying; still, they believe sharing their experiences is the best way to take you, the reader, into their journey.

We are grateful for their dedication and commitment, and we encourage you to emulate their approach to "overcome" as you consider your journey.

Special thanks to:
Prof. Juanita Illingworth
Jonathan Buffard
Vjollca Behuli
Benjamin Samuel
Armando Licoze
Ann Austin
Gary Chandler
Martin Imlach
Carey-Ann Thurlow
Dr. Kieran Mervyn
Rohan Johnson
Angela Russell Grier
Angeliki Papasava

Julie Bagley

Warren Dix

Elizabeth Johnson

Jameika Green

Jonathan Bossaer

Ray Brennan

Dr Nii Amoo

Divine Orji

THANK YOU!

CHAPTER ONE

TRANSFORMING OBSTACLES INTO STEPPING STONES

by Jonathan Buffard

At work, as in life, we constantly face obstacles and challenges that test our resilience, adaptability, and determination. These experiences shape us as individuals and leaders, teaching us invaluable lessons and providing growth opportunities. As someone with a natural riches-to-rags upbringing, I have had my fair share of change and setbacks.

My ability to adapt, pivot, and overcome obstacles has defined my success and shaped the person and leader I am today. You've heard to not rest on your laurels, but an even better lesson is not to get hung up on your failures and on things you can't control.

I have encountered numerous challenges throughout my life, each teaching me a lesson about perseverance and adaptability. Some of the biggest obstacles leaders face in various spheres of life stem from self-doubt and impostor syndrome, the rapidly changing landscapes of our fields, and the uncertain and daunting future in a world of artificial intelligence (AI) and technological innovations. However, our perception of ourselves may differ from how others see us and how overcoming adversity can strengthen our character and leadership abilities.

Insights from famous leaders and principles from ancient philosophies like Taoism will help to guide you while navigating the complexities of leadership and embracing change as an opportunity for growth.

In the process of becoming the leader you are meant to be, investigating the roles of passion, interests, uncertainty, and circumstance in shaping our professional lives is fundamental to developing emotional intelligence, self-awareness, and growth, along with the importance of striking a balance between ambition and contentment becomes indispensable qualities that contribute to overcoming challenges and becoming a better version of yourself over time.

OVERCOME

"Vincit Qui Se Vincit"

The greatest challenge we face in life is often not external circumstances or other people but our internal battles. At the heart of this struggle lies self-doubt, a pervasive and sometimes crippling force that can hinder our progress and prevent us from realizing our full potential.

The Latin phrase "Vincit Qui Se Vincit" - He Conquers Who Conquers Himself - is a powerful reminder that the most significant victories are often achieved within SELF and have been that way throughout history. Self-doubt is an emotion that can strike anyone, regardless of their achievements or standing. It is estimated that around 70% of people have experienced impostor syndrome at some point in their lives, a phenomenon characterised by a persistent belief that one's accomplishments are not deserved and that one is a fraud waiting to be exposed. Even some of the most successful individuals have admitted to experiencing self-doubt and impostor syndrome. For example, Meryl Streep once shared that before she starts a new movie, **"I say to myself, 'I don't know how to act — and why does anybody want to look at me on-screen anymore?' ... Lots of actors feel that way. What gives you strength is also your weakness — your raging insecurity."**

I like this quote because it reveals two important lessons. First, even the best have self-doubt, and second, the key lies in turning that weakness into a strength. Overcoming self-doubt requires a combination of self-awareness, self-compassion, and persistence. It involves recognizing that we are not alone in our inadequacy and that even the most accomplished individuals struggle with doubt. To conquer ourselves, we must first understand the root causes of our self-doubt, whether from past experiences, societal pressures, or a natural predisposition towards anxiety and insecurity. Don't let your impostor syndrome keep you from trying. Let it instead keep you hungry and humble, feeding your need to ever-improve.

Another critical aspect of overcoming self-doubt is seeking support from others, whether it be through mentors, friends, or professional help. Sharing our experiences and vulnerabilities can help us accept feelings of inadequacy and foster a sense of camaraderie, allowing us to recognize that we are not alone in our struggles. Moreover, seeking guidance from those we admire or who have experienced similar challenges can provide invaluable insights into conquering our self-doubt and growing as individuals.

If you suffer from impostor syndrome, don't worry; you're in good company. Tom Hanks, Michelle Obama, Arianna Huffington, and Serena Williams have all admitted to feeling the same way. Chances are, some of the people you most admire in your work and life feel the same way you do. It's fascinating that even individuals celebrated as the best in their fields can be plagued by self-doubt. Reflecting on my personal experiences, I recall always considering myself shy. This self-perception greatly influenced my actions and fears. It was when I turned 30 that I grasped the truth.

A close friend confided her anxiety during social interactions and her battle with shyness. "Impossible!" I exclaimed, "You're incredibly outgoing! I'm the shy one!" To my astonishment, she perceived me as bold and confident, just as I saw her. Over time, similar conversations with outgoing people revealed two crucial insights: our self-perception doesn't always align with others' views, and those who appear extroverted might be striving harder to overcome their feelings of shyness. This leads us to our next lesson: overcoming and embracing the growth mindset.

GROWTH Vs FIXED MINDSET

As defined by psychologist Carol Dweck, a growth mindset is the belief that one's intelligence, talents, and abilities can be developed and enhanced through dedication, effort, and learning from experiences. Dweck states, "*In a growth mindset, people believe that their most basic abilities can be developed through dedication and hard work—brains and talent are just the starting point.*" This perspective contrasts with a fixed mindset, where individuals believe their traits and abilities are static and unchangeable. The importance of a growth mindset lies in the understanding that virtually no one is born with innate skills or predispositions. Skills are cultivated through consistent practice and hard work, meaning anyone can develop and improve in any area.

A study conducted by Dweck revealed that students with a growth mindset outperformed those with a fixed mindset, even when they began with equal abilities. This demonstrates how the power of belief in personal growth can significantly impact one's success and development. Embracing a growth mindset is essential for overcoming adversity, working on oneself, and achieving personal and professional growth. This mindset fosters resilience, encouraging individuals to view challenges and setbacks as opportunities to learn and improve. According to a report by Harvard Business Review, people with a growth mindset are 34% more likely to make a positive behavior change, such as setting and achieving goals or overcoming obstacles. By adopting a growth mindset, individuals become more open to feedback, committed to learning, and capable of adapting to change, all contributing to a lifelong journey of self-improvement and success.

THE TAO OF WORK

Overcoming adversity is essential to personal and professional growth, allowing individuals to build resilience and develop a positive mindset. One way to overcome adversity is by incorporating the principles of Taoism in leadership. Taoism, an ancient Chinese philosophy, emphasises harmony, balance, and living by natural flow. By applying these principles, leaders can better navigate challenges and foster a more adaptable and resilient mindset. Going with the flow is a core tenet of Taoism and involves embracing the natural course of events rather than resisting them. When individuals adopt this approach, they can more effectively respond to change and make informed decisions based on the current circumstances. This flexibility allows for a more adaptable leadership style, where unexpected situations are seen as opportunities for growth and learning rather than threats; thus, time is not wasted mourning for things we have no control over. *By going with the flow, you'll spend less time worrying about how things used to be and more time making the best of whatever situation you find yourself in.*

Following the path of least resistance is another valuable principle derived from Taoism. This concept encourages individuals to pursue their goals and ambitions while remaining mindful of their environment and feelings. Lao Tzu noted, "A good traveller has no fixed plans and is not intent on arriving." By understanding and adapting to the world around them, leaders can create an environment where success is more attainable, and progress is made with fewer obstacles, keeping in mind that the journey matters. Embracing change as an opportunity is essential for overcoming adversity. Lao Tzu's wisdom on change is evident in his words, "When I let go of what I am, I become what I might be." This means leaving preconceived notions at the door and opening yourself up for change and growth.

When leaders view change as a chance to grow, innovate, and evolve, they can inspire their teams to adopt a similar mindset, fostering a culture of continuous improvement where setbacks are viewed as learning experiences and opportunities to strengthen the organisation or aid in their transformation. Learning from failures is crucial for developing resilience and overcoming adversity. Lao Tzu recognised the importance of learning from mistakes, saying, "Failure is the foundation of success and how it is achieved." By treating failures as valuable lessons, leaders can cultivate a growth mindset and inspire their teams to do the same, driving personal and organizational growth. Resilience and developing a positive mindset are vital for overcoming adversity in leadership. Lao Tzu's words on resilience ring true today: "The bamboo that bends is stronger than the oak that resists."

When leaders exhibit resilience, they demonstrate their ability to bounce back from setbacks and remain steadfast in facing challenges. This resilience and a growth mindset create an environment where teams feel empowered to take risks, explore new ideas, and grow personally and professionally. By incorporating principles of Taoism and fostering a culture of resilience, leaders can more effectively navigate adversity and create a lasting impact on their organisations. Overcome adversity by adapting to it and becoming a better version of yourself.

BECOME

Think about what you wanted to be as a child. Think about what you wanted to be in high school. What did you study in college? What's your job today? What would you like to do? Most likely, the answers to these questions are not the same. Becoming who we are as leaders and professionals involves personal passion, interests, uncertainty, and circumstance. Throughout our lives, we encounter various experiences and opportunities that shape our personal and professional development, ultimately influencing the people and leaders we become.

Passion and interests play a significant role in our growth, depending on how encouraged we are to develop and pursue them. When deeply passionate about a subject or field, we tend to invest more time and energy into mastering the skills and knowledge associated with it. Our interests guide us toward specific career paths, pushing us to excel and contribute meaningfully to our chosen fields.

However, fate and circumstance also play a crucial part in our development. Chance encounters, unexpected opportunities, and life-changing events can lead us to explore new avenues or shift our focus entirely, ultimately contributing to the evolution of our professional identity. The key is to strike a balance between the two. Don't just accept a career path because it's the one that presented itself to you, and you've been going on autopilot ever since. Be open to growth and change. On the other hand, don't consistently veer off your path either. If you constantly find yourself back on the same career path, perhaps it's for a reason. Understanding yourself, your desires, and your motivations is critical to finding harmony between the two. This leads us to emotional intelligence (EI), another critical factor in shaping who we are as leaders and professionals. EI refers to our ability to recognise, understand, and manage our own emotions, as well as the feelings of others.

EI is essential for building solid relationships, effectively communicating, and navigating complex social dynamics in the workplace. Leaders with high emotional intelligence are likelier to empathise with their team members, understand their needs, and create a supportive work environment that fosters productivity and satisfaction. Self-awareness and personal growth are integral components of our journey as leaders and professionals and are crucial to understanding if your career path results from happenstance or personal desire. By recognising our strengths and weaknesses, we can actively work towards self-improvement and continuous growth. Self-awareness allows us to identify areas where we excel and areas that require further development, enabling us to pursue opportunities that align with our capabilities and interests.

As we grow personally and professionally, our leadership style and approach to problem-solving evolve, allowing us to adapt and thrive in diverse situations. Managing expectations is another crucial aspect of our development as leaders and professionals. It involves setting realistic goals for ourselves and our teams, understanding the limitations and constraints of various situations, and adjusting our expectations as circumstances change.

Influential leaders recognise the importance of balancing ambition with pragmatism, ensuring that goals are achievable while challenging others and themselves to push the boundaries of what is possible. We can't all be Elon Musk, nor should we aim to be. Managing expectations about your career is essential. What does success look like to you? Do you have a realistically reasonable goal? Ambition is the fire that burns within, but if you're not careful, it'll burn down your whole life. Don't be ambitious for the sake of it; use ambition to gain fulfillment. Be aware of what being overly ambitious will do to your quality of life. Nobody has ever been on their deathbed saying, "I wish I would have spent more time at work!" Keep that in mind as you think about what success means for you.

In short, becoming who we are as leaders and professionals is shaped by passion, interests, fate, circumstance, emotional intelligence, self-awareness, and our ability to manage expectations and adapt to change. By embracing these factors and continuously striving for growth, we can become a person of influence, a leader, a role model, and the professionals we are meant to be. When all is said and done, the journey of overcoming and becoming personally or professionally transformed is challenging yet rewarding. Every hardship faced is an opportunity for growth, and every success is a testament to resilience and adaptability. Let's remember the words of John F. Kennedy (JFK), who said, "Change is the law of life. And those who look only to the past or present will surely miss the future." This statement encapsulates the essence of this chapter — the need for continuous learning, adaptability, and the courage to embrace change.

Consider the case of J. K. Rowling, who faced numerous rejections from publishers before the fame of the Harry Potter series. Despite the odds, she persevered, and her story serves as an example of tenacity and determination. Her quote, "It is impossible to live without failing at something unless you live so cautiously that you might as well not have lived at all - in which case, you fail by default," speaks volumes about embracing failure as a stepping stone towards success. From a statistical perspective, according to a report by McKinsey & Company, companies that prioritise innovation and adaptability are 1.7 times more likely to outperform their industry peers in terms of profit margin. These companies foster an environment that promotes learning, encourages creativity, and celebrates success. They understand the importance of enabling others to grow and develop their ambitions, creating a more engaged and motivated workforce.

Remember the words of Richard Branson, "Do not be embarrassed by your failures; learn from them and start again." Overcoming is the first step, and becoming is the subsequent journey. The path may be laden with obstacles, but armed with perseverance, adaptability, and a growth mindset, you can navigate it successfully. As you embark on your next journey, I hope you will take these lessons to heart and apply them in your personal and professional endeavours. Finally, yet importantly, I hope that the insights and lessons shared in this book and my personal experiences will help you overcome obstacles in your own life and inspire you to become the leader you are meant to be.

By embracing change, learning from our experiences, and fostering a culture of growth and collaboration, we can all rise to the challenge and make a lasting impact in our personal and professional lives.

CHAPTER TWO

BREAKING BARRIERS: ACHIEVING YOUR DREAMS

by Vjollca Behuli

PART I

Nowadays, the word that we hear so often is LEADERSHIP. I wonder what people imagine when they hear this word. Despite the advanced development of Information Technology trends, this word presents a different image in everyone's head. But the speed of the information was not the same many years ago when I was a little girl. So, when I heard the word LEADERSHIP, I imagined it to be a very complex process with high integrity and trustworthiness.

I have always imagined that for one to be a Leader, that person should be resilient in many aspects, be kind with great heart and integrity, one that others would serve as a role model, that others can trust and follow with no doubts. I am saying this as that's how my father was. Now, my father was an ordinary citizen in the small town of Gjilan. At that time, part of the socialist country Yugoslavia[1] comprised six constituent republics and two autonomous provinces, one of which was Kosovo, my home country. He used to work in a large public trade company, and even though he was just a clerk, he learned leadership and taught us how important it is to be strong and contribute to the country in which we live.

Learning leadership in his challenging life has been crucial for the family's survival. We lived in a family of six: three sisters, a brother, and our parents. But in 1994, my father succumbed to chronic heart disease at age 52. He was a hard worker and dedicated all his life to this country and his family. I remember when I was a little girl, he would spend most of his time in the hospital under the doctor's care, sometimes up to three months in a row. He was so energetic that upon his release from the hospital, one would find him already working in the garden the next day.

We were very young when he passed; hence, all the burden of the family welfare was now on my mother's and brother's shoulders, the eldest child in the family, who was only 22 then. I have always longed to have him by my side so he can see what a good-hearted person I have become and be proud of me. He never saw my achievements, but deep in my heart, I believe he is watching me from above.

At the time of my father's passing, I was studying to become a primary education teacher and graduated only a few months later. Upon graduating in the second half of 1994, I was already looking for a job. In 1995, I had the opportunity to work at a primary school in my hometown, Gjilan, for a maternity replacement period of nine months. I got so enthusiastic about working with kids that I would not sleep at night, thinking of how to make my class the top performer in the school. Unfortunately, the previous teacher was not very dedicated; therefore, I saw I had a long way to go to reach this goal. By this time, we were left in poverty, as my country was going through a challenging political situation, leading to war shortly after. Hence, I was using this very little money to support my family.

The financial circumstances of the students in my class could have been better, so I came up with the idea of engaging everyone to make the lessons more attractive so that even those weak students would pass the class. I coordinated with parents, and we devised the idea to cover the teaching materials jointly, which would be used in the class so that students would feel included. And this worked very well. I balanced the teaching methods with the parents' collaboration to make it all-inclusive.

In my class, this little girl came to school daily with the same clothes torn apart. Her hair was messy, her face quite dirty, and her school bag almost empty. She had no books, no notebooks, only a few worn-down pencils. Not that others were in a better situation, except for one or two, but this one was in bad shape.

And soon comes July 1996, the end of the school year. The school had this tradition of taking a joint class photo in memory of the school year. They would bring a photographer to school one day, ask all the teachers to line up with their students, take a joint photo, then print the pictures and distribute them to the students. If the students could not make the payment, they wouldn't receive their photos. Did I mention earlier that I was with no dimes at this point? So, I prepared my class for the joint kind of family photo. We went outside in the garden, and I lined them up, the smaller ones sitting in front, the more prominent students standing in the back.

The photographer takes the photo and says he will deliver the photos in a week. I am supposed to collect the money from the kids to give to the photographer when he brings the photos. While I collected the money during the day, another kid said, Miss Vjollca, Rita, the girl I just mentioned, has no money to pay for the picture, so all the kids in the class will pay for her photo. And that's when she burst into tears and said, *"No, no, my Mum has gone to the neighbours this morning to borrow the money so I can pay for the photo. I don't know how she will pay them back, as we have no income, but she told me not to worry"*.

So, at this moment, I burst into tears, and I ran to the office of the school principal to seek support, just to be amazed by his reaction and accusations that I was crossing the line by going against the school rules, hence, he has no choice but to let me go, once my contract ended.

PART II

I lost my first job when my country was in a recession period. My country, Kosovo, belongs to the former Republic of Yugoslavia[1], one of the two autonomous provinces. Due to political upheavals and conflicts, the Republic of Yugoslavia dissolved in 1991- 1992[2]. Serbia initiated a dispute with six Republics of former Yugoslavia and Kosovo as autonomous province[2]. Kosovo has suffered a recession for ten years, which ended with an armed conflict in 1999. During this recession, all the Kosovar Albanians were expelled from their jobs and given little to no rights in public services. People were on the verge of hunger and could only work in the private sector, which was highly underdeveloped at this time.

One of the major sources of income for Albanians was from the diaspora. How-ever, owing to the extraordinary situation, people had difficulty traveling and sending money to support their families. These limitations also affected the education sector by closing all the schools, forcing people to find alternatives by converting their houses into schools for kids. After I lost my first job in 1996, I had this utmost need to support my family financially since no one else was working. So, I started to work on and sell traditional handcrafts for young brides and to sustain my family's well-being. In the meantime, I got a job offer from my close relative to work as a shop assistant in a shoe shop.

I gladly accepted this job, as I knew this would provide my family and me with a sustainable income. Little did I know that working in a shop is less attractive than it appears. The political situation in my country worsened, and Serbia had already increased its military presence in the city. I worked six days a week with customers and did a general cleaning of the shop every Sunday, so I had no day off. However, working at this shop did have its bright side, as I would have plenty of time to read and the opportunity to meet many people and create many friendships.

I read all kinds of books and literature, anything that would come to my hand. Later in my career, I realised that reading during this time had created a treasure in my brain that I utilised later in many aspects of life. I continued working at the shoe shop for about two years, 1997–1999, the most challenging time of my life. The mere presence of a team of paramilitary forces stationed in front of the entry to the shop was intimidating. At their liberty, they would stop customers, mainly men, ask them questions, and sometimes even physically assault them as they had to pass them. For me, however, the scariest time would be Sundays, when I had to go and clean the shop. The roads were almost empty, yet they would hang in front of my shop. Every Sunday, I imagined being shot or tortured by them. Luckily, nothing happened, but I constantly feared it for nearly two years.

PART III

With the entry of KFOR Military forces in Kosovo in June 1999[3], we finally got liberated after ten years of recession and a period of armed conflict through the Kosovo Liberation Army. I forgot earlier that my Mum got sick about three weeks before the liberation during the armed conflict and needed urgent surgery. She had surgery in the hospital, and she returned home. For Mum, the road to recovery was quite long and challenging, so my brother, sister, and I took turns taking care of her while my second sister got married in 1998 and went to Switzerland with her husband.

As soon as the conflict ended, my sister traveled from Switzerland to come and visit. She received very different news during this period and was unsure that the family was still alive. Meeting us for the first time was very emotional; I will never forget it. With my sister here, we would spend our days outside in the garden, ensuring Mum had everything she needed. Most of the time, we would also discuss our future and how things would be for us, and my sister was trying to put us at ease by confirming that she would be there for us. However, this could have been more comforting, so I started looking for jobs. By this time, Kosovo was on the mend with international organisations looking for local staff members, but to this end, I had yet to find anything. One day, as I was in the kitchen cooking for the family, my sister came in, asking that I go outside and meet a group of people asking for some directions, but because they were speaking English, they needed help translating. So, I went outside and met this group of people from the Czech Republic through Czech Caritas[4] to help build schools. They were looking for a location to attend a coordination meeting, so I said I would be glad to take them there.

On the way to the location, they told me they had brought an Albanian translator who spoke Czech, but upon arrival, he wanted to continue working, so they were looking for a translator. They asked me if I would like to start working with them, against a daily rate of €20, as they thought my English was quite good. I thought for a moment, accepted the offer, and knew I had made the right decision. This decision has followed me through my entire career hereafter, and I believe it set my path towards building my professional life, for which I thank God, who made my road enlighten and set to follow for all these years.

PART IV

I worked with Czech Caritas for less than a year, building schools, helping those in need, supporting hospitals, and coordinating aid for the people of

Kosovo. At the end of the armed conflict, 85% of the country was burnt and destroyed. Immediately after the liberation in June 1999, the people forced to flee their homes were returning to nowhere, so their only hope was support and assistance from the International Community. By this time, however, the role and mission of the International Community was nearing its end.

In February 2000, there was an opening with the United Nations Mission in Kosovo[5], the largest international community in Kosovo, that was working on establishing the Administration Structures for the position of Language Assistant. I applied for that position, knowing that the salary was good and that I needed financial aid to support my family. In my mind, if I got the job, which was hard, with the country just recovering and with an unemployment rate of over 80%, I would stay for a short period of about three to six months, make some money, and then find my way back to teaching in school. Interestingly, I always dreamed of becoming a teacher, a dream shared by my late father.

Anyway, by this time, my mother's health had started to improve, and she had become a guide in my life and career. I have tried all my life to pay her back with my good deeds for her remarkable contribution in continuing her guidance and filling in for my father since his loss in 1994 until today, and I always have this feeling that nothing I do is truly enough. Okay, back to the story of UNMIK. I did get a job as a Language Assistant with them and started working in February 2000, and this is when the real challenges in my career began.

For the record, I did not study English, nor had any English training or courses taken when I started working with the UNMIK Municipal Administrator, Mr. Bob Symons. Before coming to Kosovo, Mr. Symons served as the chief executive officer of the Daventry Council. He is the hardest-working person I have ever met. I have always felt fortunate to have worked with him, as I got the best practice of my life, personally and professionally. So, my plan to work for about three to six months with UNMIK lasted nearly five years, setting the stage for my professional career development and guiding me throughout my life. I was working on establishing municipal structures for the first time after the armed conflict. After the change in the system, we were transitioning from a Socialist to a Democratic country. My role in the UNMIK administration started to expand, not only to provide language assistance in the meetings, conferences, assemblies, etc., but I was getting involved more in the content of the administration, from the legal, financial, and technical aspects.

Slowly but steadily, I developed personally in a very challenging political environment. I started supporting the municipality in drafting different legal acts and regulations, documents and certifications, financial and budgetary planning, and strategic planning. So, my first role in more of an institutional field allowed me to expose myself to the political and administrative world and grow and mature as a professional. Nevertheless, as Kosovo as a state was moving towards the transitional period, taking over the decision-making and administrative role of the International Community by taking responsibility for leading the country, UNMIK's function was slowly fading.

By this time, I had already started looking for other options and alternatives to continue my career development. It was in early 2005 that I attended the Board of Directors meeting with my supervisor. During this meeting, I saw two new faces also participating, whom the Chief Executive Officer of the Gjilan municipality introduced as representatives of the new USAID project on Local Governance, who were there to launch the beginning of this project. They would occupy the same building as the mayor, working directly in their advisory role to support the municipality and the country to transition in the leadership system towards a direct mayoral election, who would have all the political and executive power. At the end of the meeting, an American guy, Mr. Richard Kobayashi, approached me, requesting a coffee. I gladly accepted the invitation, and we went to a nearby coffee shop for a quick coffee. Mr. Kobayashi expressed his interest in having me join his team in the Municipal Management Consultant role, which was an exciting offer for me.

I came home and consulted with my mother and brother, who thought this would be an excellent opportunity to change my development path. I decided to try it and go through the application procedure. A few days later, I interviewed for the position and signed a contract. I started working with USAID in June 2005. I was thrilled and looking forward to this new challenge ahead. I worked mainly on the content directly with high municipal officials and gained new perspectives and experience. I would meet the Mayor of Gjilan municipality daily and support his work in any way possible. That put me in a trusted position, and the mayor and the rest of the municipal administration highly respected me.

One day in 2006, during our regular exchange with the mayor, he said, *"I want the citizens of my municipality to have one place in the administration to obtain all their services."* I looked at Mr. Kobayashi, and he said, *"What you need is a one-stop shop, all-in-one services place, and we will help you put together a concept and support the establishment of the facility, training of the staff and functionalisation".* After this meeting, he put together a team of people. We worked together to establish the One-Stop-Shop, the first facility of this kind in Kosovo, followed by all the other 38 municipalities in Kosovo as a good practice and example.

On another typical day in the office in 2006, while having our morning macchiato, Mr. Kobayashi said, "Vjollca, the local election is approaching very soon. I would like to see Kosovo transform its election system towards the Direct Election of the Mayor. One good example could be the practice of the Executive Mayor system in Boston, Massachusetts. How about having you go to Boston on an internship and learn more about this structure." I was staring at him, not knowing what to say. This idea came out of nowhere, and I was shocked. I did not know whether I could hold that type of responsibility. I was scared to say a word and wasn't even sure what an internship was. I was hearing this for the first time in my life.

Mr. Kobayashi talked about this great opportunity and how he would present this project to USAID, seek their financial support for my stay in the United States of America, and offer me to stay at his place in Boston and how I would enjoy going there. Things developed so fast, so before I knew it, I had already received an invitation letter from Mayor Menino (RIP), and I was on a plane to the USA. During my one-month internship with the office of Mayor Menino, I worked directly with Mrs. Robin Hadley, the first advisor to the mayor. She assisted me in attending meetings, conferences, and seminars, interviewing people, sightseeing, and going to the theatre and cinema. I even went to New York on the weekend. On my return from the USA, I drafted a report, which was submitted to the Kosovo institutions by the USAID as a good practice in preparing Law on Local Government Administration in 2007, by which Law Kosovo changed its election system to move towards the Direct Election of the Mayor with Executive Power. So, this was my vast achievement, giving me a significant turn in my career development.

PART V

My outstanding contribution to the first USAID project on Local Governance opened the road for me to continue working with two projects from 2008–2013. However, I oriented more toward a management role, working as the Grants Manager. I found the new position challenging and rewarding in thinking about my current development path and balancing it with my academic development. When the successor of USAID Effective Municipalities Initiative[6] started with implementation, the new project manager, Mr. Gabriel Abraham, was talking to me about my great potential, energy, and enthusiasm.

He brought up my education and how a Master's degree would further enhance my opportunities towards more competence-based roles in the future. By then, I had graduated from the University of Education to become a teacher. Finally, my dream of becoming a teacher was coming true. However, as time passed, I started seeing myself as more acquainted with public administration rather than teaching. I already had some years of experience and felt comfortable doing what I was doing. Even though he continuously kept reminding me of my further education, I was still deciding whether to leave my job for my studies due to my family obligations.

My mother was getting older, and she needed constant care. She had already developed diabetes and was suffering from hypertension and osteoporosis. I continued to work with USAID until 2013, when I decided I needed a change. I had already done my seven years in three projects in a row and felt that my work had become a routine, and I had no more contribution. At this point, I had started to think more seriously about my future academic development and had been researching the potential Universities to do a Master's degree. Given my several years of experience as a Grants Manager, I had already oriented myself toward a Project Management field of study.

Even though I was in between jobs, I was still thinking of the possibility of a University that would enable distance learning. This way, I would be close to home for my family and study on my path. In April 2013, my application was finally successful. I got accepted to a Project Management program with Roehampton University in London, UK, a three-year program suitable for working people so they could study during their available time. And this worked very well for me. I completed my studies in 2016 and graduated with a Master's in Project Management. The studying time was not easy, but with the great team of staff from the University, professors, mentors during my thesis research, and the invaluable support from my family, it has been a rewarding experience. I feel so honored and proud to have had the opportunity to be part of this journey.

PART VI

My Master's studies at the University of Roehampton have set the stage for my professional and academic development. I have gained the best experience that has followed me since my growth. I see things differently and have a different approach to my professional life. I have mentioned several times that my professional focus had shifted from my forever dream of teaching to my forever contribution to public administration (I have already worked for 20 years in public administration).

In the last couple of years, I have been thinking about how I have worked in the public sector and how it would be great to institutionalise this experience and practice through research, allowing new generations to utilize it in the future. Moreover, I realized that Local Governance is my area of interest, and I want to explore the field further. With this in mind, I started doing my second Master's degree in Local Governance at my hometown's University "Kadri Zeka'. Currently, I am doing my thesis, which focuses on Electronic Procurement as one of the pressing issues in Kosovo. My ambition is to set the basis for better management of public funding in my country.

CHAPTER THREE

THE QUAKES OF LIFE

by Benjamin Samuel

THE 1ST QUAKE

How does that one deserving to be called a leader handle issues associated with **Self?** One must deal with anger, hopelessness, distrust, conspiracy theories, conflicts, crises, mistakes, and losses meticulously. To attain that point, one must adequately take control when these situations arise, especially when one, two or more people are involved. Every true leader must have gone through one inspirational experience or another (that at first seems like a tipping point) to be capable of taking control when it comes to others. For instance, in my home, I am a leader. The intricacies of leading my family must stem from my experiences with my birth family or my experiences with others, but most definitely from my life experiences.

I have been called a leader outside my home and in standing true to my desire. However, I feel experiences alone don't automatically make one a leader.

Instead, the willingness to fill that role when leadership is required and the ability to take from that experience and use it to empower someone else – for me, that is authentic leadership. However, let me share a few of my experiences with you and let you judge how I feel about being a leader.

My early years in tertiary institution felt like a bird let out of the nest to come face to face with its prey. In 1998 (18 years of age and gullible), I finally got admission into Kaduna Polytechnic, Kaduna State, Nigeria, to study Urban and Regional Planning. After flunking badly with my O-Level, I had to start with a remedial class called PRE-ND. With mixed feelings about staying in a cousin's BQ who worked with the institution, I got my Dad to permit me to stay in a rented apartment near my campus (10 minutes away). I shared the room (a big hall-looking kind of room) with three other students introduced to me by a long-time secondary school friend studying architecture with the institution. What I can say about these three friends is that they were bad influences.

One time, I got some money from my cousin sent to me by my Dad. These friends took advantage of my generosity, methodically got me drunk, and stole all I had in my pocket. I woke up to realise that their being nice was fiendish, which prompted me to leave them and stay with my long-time secondary school friend (Martin Buden), who introduced me to them. A lovely Catholic widow, his mother, accepted me in their home and made me feel very welcome.

So, not too long into staying with Martin, towards the end of the year, around December of 1998, I got a call from my elder brother asking me to come home because my Dad wanted to see me. I wondered why my Dad would summon me from school (being such an Educationist that he was) until I got home and saw that my Dad was under hospital admission. I was dumbfounded. He looked different, despite quite his handsome self, but completely weak. He did not speak to me as such but held my hand for a long time, say 20 to 30 minutes, before letting me go. I remember praying in the hospital. When

I went home, I prayed hard, looking forward to the next day when I would go again to see my Dad. The next day, my Mum returned home crying that my Dad had passed. He died on December 29, 1998, at the age of 50. Quake number one rocked my entire being.

THE 2nd QUAKE

Before his death, Dad had been working in a steel merchant company, not just that but including all other sorts of trade/services like computer services and equipment, knitting services, alcoholic beverages, and other merchandising services (as depicted in the Articles and Memorandum of Association). Dad registered the company, signed up his wife and children on the board of directors, and worked out his modalities of how the company would swing into action. He was waiting for his self-willed resignation to be approved. We all had discussions concerning the company at a family meeting and signed our undertakings for the legal aspect.

I remember what Dad said: if he died, we were unlikely to meet the demands of daily survival compared to some Fulani boys and girls sent by their parents out to hawk groundnuts, groundnut cakes, and other trivial things, perishable merchandise. His excuse was! ***"You don't have the kind of survival training these children have. "*** It was a worry for me because I felt like my Dad had undermined the capacity of his children. When he died, I was devastated. The company died a natural death despite my little, helpless efforts, but in my mind, I felt my Dad had won, considering our conversation.

Later in life, it would occur that my Dad (knowingly or unknowingly) played a key leadership role by challenging us to bring out the best in us. Before you conclude judgment on this, let me finish the narrative. So, time went by, and school progressed. I had agreed to stay in my cousin's BQ and focus more on my studies under his watchful eyes. I was in my ND 1 last semester, looking forward to my exams, then ND II, getting a job and preparing myself for the next phase in education. That was in 1999, the year I got baptised (immersed in the death of Christ and resurrected with him to a new life).

I bring this up because my Religious Faith played and still plays a crucial role in helping me go through the quakes that rocked my life experiences. To get back to my narrative to the point where exams came around the corner: -preparatory readings and revisions had to commence. During my studies as an ND 1 student in the College of Environmental Studies, Department of Town and Urban Planning, I made friends – we all do; it is a norm in life. So, as I was saying, preparatory to exams for the next class, ND II, Friday, Obaje and I became study mates (friends), and Obaje made it wax strong because he probably saw the prospects of doing well by tagging along with a friend.

Well, Obaje – he had money (his father had money, a Secret Security Service SSS personnel), and I had brains. All said and done, our last paper will be a borrowed course called ICT (Information Communication Technology). To Obaje, that was a nightmare and later would become mine. Despite all the confidence I made him feel during the eve of the paper and his observed readiness, Obaje would not let me be in the examination hall. I was last on the column we sat, and his seat was before mine, with other seats ahead of him and other columns to our left and right.

Obaje bombarded me to help him answer a fourth and the last question because he had been able to answer three. To help him complete his fourth question – (a mandatory number of questions to answer) – I wrote the answers on the back of my question paper, exchanged them with him, and left the hall to submit my answer script. As it turned out, that was the biggest mistake I have ever made in my educational pursuit. The next day, while working on completing my last studio work in ND 1, my friend Awal came up to the U-block accompanied by a stranger. He needed my attention and asked me to come along. From our short conversation, Obaje had passed the question paper with my answer to someone, that someone to another someone, until the next someone was spotted passing it to another by the institution's Secret Security, positioned at a strategic corner outside the exam hall.

That was devastating news but not devastating enough to rock my being. So, the exam malpractice board will explain their strategy: *"We noticed your handwriting on this question paper according to your colleagues because the ink and handwriting on their answer scripts do not match this. "How did your question paper get to them?"* That was the moment that my self-resolve got tested. Out of the people who got caught and dragged to the malpractice panel, Obaje was not among them. I needed clarification. They did not accept my answer, **"I don't know."**

I asked their permission to relieve myself in the bathroom, and when I entered the toilet, I immediately went on my knees and prayed to GOD to help me speak the truth because HE said in HIS word that the truth would set me free. I wish I could learn of your thoughts on this final act of mine because when I got back to the malpractice panel, I told them I had given my question paper to Obaje. *Great tidings! Obaje denied ever knowing me in his life – he swore to GOD.* My cousin, the chairman of the examination malpractice board and owner of the BQ where I stayed, was contacted. He signed the rustication for all the culprits, including someone who just passed the question paper as a help and including me, his cousin.

Quake number two rocked my entire being, and it got worse when I told my mother after I got back home from Kaduna, feeling dejected and at my tipping point. She wept on her knees the whole night.

THE 3rd QUAKE

Again, my father's words came back, sneering at me. In the year 2000, 20 years of age, I got fed up with nothing to do but gobble up mom's delicious cooking.

We once visited my elder sister Oneshi in Mararaba (a border town between Nasarawa state and Abuja, the Federal Capital Territory). We stayed a few days, and on the departure day, I carried several things: a few books, clothes, and other stuff in polyethylene bags. I am sure my Mum noticed me struggling as we approached the road where we would board vehicles back to Jos, the Plateau State Capital. I tried to stuff the smaller bags into bigger ones, and it was not working. It was irritating, frustrating, and annoying. You could tell from my face that I was not friendly.

My Mum held me and collected the more oversized bag, removed those other bags I had stuffed in, and did something I still could not understand. She gently held it open and said, ***"Don't ever give up"***, as she motioned me to put the bags in my hand. They fit in snugly, and as the others followed, they also fit in snugly and left me with one bag (my idea that I tried helplessly to achieve) to carry instead of several. Those words from my Mum stirred something in me that has, until today, been a jump-starter cable between me and anything that tries to make me feel depleted in life. I will never give up.

Still, within the year 2000, not far from when we got back from my sister's, I took a solo and unannounced trip to Kaduna. I went straight to my cousin's office; I did not even bother to go to his house (my second home). He was stricken when he saw me. He asked what brought me there and clarified that I would dance to the music I had played earlier.

Being a dedicated Muslim, before I left Kaduna, I went into his home to beg him, and he told me all the ***dance-to-your-music stuff,*** insisting I release him so he could go and observe his evening prayers. He was disgusted and never took a second look at me. This time around, in his office, it was nothing near prayer time; nevertheless, I went on my knees and begged him to give me a second chance. I told him my motive was to help and never carried any contraband material into the exam hall. He responded, *"If you need to help* *someone, help him outside the exam hall; inside the exam hall, if you help someone, it is considered examination malpractice."* True! How stupid to forget a tiny thing that could have kept me out of such big troubles. I did not relent in begging because I thought of what I had put my Mum through. I did! So, I begged for a second chance, for help.

Being the Deputy Registrar of Academics for the institution, my cousin opened his drawer and brought out an admissions application form for me (I assume he paid for it because I did not pay a dime for it). He gave me three options: Tourism, Business Administration, and Computer Science. Without equivocation, I opted for Computer Science, the borrowed course that messed up my studies in the College for Environmental Studies, Department for Town and Urban Planning. I filled out the form, gave it to him, and thanked him. A few weeks later, I was admitted to the Kaduna Polytechnic, Kaduna state, Nigeria, to study Computer Science in 2000.

I started with PRE-ND, a remedial-like class. Who cared? This was a hard-earned second chance. This time, I took it upon myself to sponsor my education and make up for my mistakes. I had made up my mind – this one was on me. My Mum got happy again; why should I bother her and my elder brother Okugya over my mistake? Well, things got good with my studies. I read and studied until I became unwell and later hospitalised. However, I was extremely good with ICT, programming, and you name it. Everything was progressing well, and I looked forward to completing my ND in Computer Science in 2004.

During those periods, whenever I have the opportunity, I take it to come home and see Mum. I recalled Mum revealing her troubling dreams of my Dad visiting her wearing his suit and beckoning her to accompany him. I remember always telling her to pray and taking her mind off it. So, just before my final session after my exams, I took one of those opportunities and decided to come home to visit my Mum.

I took the Abuja – Kaduna expressway, which is less than 2 hours to Abuja (the idea was to see my sister), then to Jos (it felt a better trip than to go from Kaduna to Jos, such a long and aching trip). Anyway, when I got to my sister's place, she told me that news had just got to her that Mum was in hospital in Aloshi, about an hour and thirty minutes from her abode. That was a bit jarring – how, when. Meanwhile, some relatives at the hospital told us our Mum had been referred to a specialist hospital in Lafia, the Nasarawa state capital.

I remember one of the relatives told me that Mum kept mentioning that she could see me on my way and that they should tell me to concentrate on my studies. That was odd since I never told her I was coming to see her. As we got to Lafia, there was no hiding it anymore. Mum had passed. She was buried in her wedding gown beside my Dad's grave the following day. Quake number three rocked my entire being.

THE 4th QUAKE

If you have not broken down, then you must keep moving. Never give up – now my keyword. How these quakes had not swallowed me, I wondered! How were my brothers and sisters coping? I asked (encouraging each other was all we had, and Okugya was the mastermind). All this while, I do not attempt to think that we were not all at our tipping points, especially me, Dad's, and Mum's favorite. My name would tell you better – Benjamin, son of the right-hand favourite child.

I recall my sister Oneshi fainting during the burial. It was all so devastating, but I had my exams to finish – something Mum would be proud of, something that would show Dad I could survive. I gathered myself together, but it was not easy. It sounds so simple to be called an orphan (to the one who refers), but to the orphan – it sounds hopeless; orphans go through awful stuff. Stuff that I eventually went through. However, I survived; I thrived because of resilience, which I am sure was fueled by my Dad, Mum, and GOD.

School resumed, and I got along very well. I got a beautiful, lovely young woman called Christiana. We were in love, and I was so fond of her. She was my classmate, and I have just now discovered why she adored me. At age 24, the thought of marriage had finally settled in. Indeed, it was my plan – a significant part of it.I remember telling the family when an older and wealthy cousin, Harry, had asked us about our plans in a family meeting, the next step after Mum passed. The final session for ND **II** came. We had finished with flying colors, and for some reason, to straighten the institution's academic calendar, we were made to continue to HND 1 almost immediately. That was 2005.

In another year, 2006, we would be graduates ready for NYSC. During our relationship, my lovely young woman and wife, as it turned out, had played the American Visa lottery at some point when she went to a café to get some stuff done.

As a big surprise to her, on the weekend, while we were taking time to relax from schoolwork, she got a call that confirmed she had won an American Visa lottery. At first, we thought it was a joke, and she even involved her uniformed brother, but we eventually realised it was true.

Throughout the remaining sessions in school, she spent time filing and signing papers until 2006, the last year – HND 2. We had finished our final exams and were looking forward to our National Youth Service Scheme (NYSC). She was busy preparing for NYSC to exempt her during the waiting period because of her travel plans. She had visited me in Jos, and my brothers Okugya and Asa were pleased to meet her.

Still unmarried and with no concrete plans to be married even in court, as advised by friends, it was a tough call for her to leave me as she openly cried over the issue. We came to terms and agreed that marriage would come after she had settled down there in the USA. *I cannot say if that is the dumbest thing I ever did. We could have married, and I could have been dependent, and I could have gone to the USA.*

She travelled back to her hometown in Adamawa, a Northern region in Nigeria, and, based on our agreement, would be back to me in Jos, then home to Abuja for her final travels. High-spirited and charismatic, Christy was always shy. She introduced me to her guardians (her aunt and uncle in Abuja), who underwent the same process. A day would not go by, and thoughts of her made me smile.

However, I was angry when I did not hear from her as agreed. She tried to explain over a phone conversation (that turned into a quarrel), but I would not listen. It would happen that she had travelled from Adamawa to Kaduna and then headed to Benue state without telling me.

After waiting a few days, I got a call from Khadijat, her friend – I had travelled and was returning. Khadijat told me that Christiana had died in a car accident on her way back from Benue State. I could not hear her anymore, and I hung up the call. I thought I was dreaming until it was later confirmed that she had died.

Quake number four rocked my entire being and left me a broken man.

THE 5th QUAKE

It does not mean you must stay down if you have broken down. Resilience – that is your guide to - Never Giving Up.

I wish I could get into details, but then NYSC helped me heal, and somehow, I overcame the guilt of being with another woman. That woman proved I could have a second go at loving someone – IV (IVerene), funny, charming, and loving. It would turn out to be a love that diverged.

Anyway, the service finished. I had hoped to be an oil boy or a banker. I had, however, applied to the Navy, Army, Airforce, Customs, Road safety, and others – in anxiety. Nothing came of it until after a few months of service, and I applied as a graduate trainee with the NNPC. Such a dream come true. I was just an oil boy.

I successfully scaled both the aptitude test and the Interview. Being in the NNPC towers was lovely, filled with oil boys and girls looking polished, intelligent, and witty. GOD, I could not wait. I had to be part of this cartel. It was a quota system, and only two of us had been picked from Nasarawa State. When given your employment letter, you are entitled to five Million Naira to clean up, as of 2008, and then attend a training school.

Documents from Abuja went to Lagos in preparation for our letters. Friends already in the cartel told us of our overwhelming success. Answered prayers, job search over –imagine it. Then the worst happened.

The Late Umaru Yaradua, then former president of Nigeria, changed the Group Managing Director of NNPC from Musa Yaradua to Barkindo (the current Secretary of OPEC). He nullified the recruitment process and decided to restructure the NNPC, so we lost employment. Quake number five shattered my dreams.

THE 6th QUAKE

It is never too late to fight back; grab the bull by the horns, toss it aside, face your demons, and make them bow. I became a drunk (what people in Nigeria will call a drunkard), drinking into a stupor. I climb into my bed filled with alcohol and empty my stomach sometimes before the alcohol is absorbed. I got a call from friends - we drink, earn money from relatives – I drink.

My sister Oneshi and I had an altercation – she called me a drunkard. I was squandering her hard-earned cash on hard liquor. Thoughts of Dad, thoughts of Mum, oh feeling so sorry for myself – I kept turning to my favourite drink. I kept at it until one faithful day when my cousin Amos invited me to meet with a family friend who worked with a Bible translation organisation.

I have had good Bible orientation from age ten - to thirteen, and I have already gained Bible certificates with the SOON Bible School, World Bible School, and others. I had read the books of Myles Munroe, T.D. Jakes, etc. Anyway, we met this man (whom I would later know as Akilla and who also became my supervisor) who was fuelling his car using a hose stuck in the fuel hole after refuelling. He had battled with it while we discussed it very informally. I, however, later suggested to him to push the hose back all the way and then pull it back slowly – it worked; the hose came out freely. Automatically, he told my cousin that I had the job.

Akilla introduced me to Mrs. Heidi (a loving mother bear, as I referred to her), an American woman with so much love (I have tears in my eyes). Hold on – I failed her! I left. She did not want me to. I think maybe she cried when I left. She used to call me her right-hand man and taught me to love GOD again. I served as an intern under her. Less than a month into the job, she arranged for me to have training with her in Kenya.

Anyway, at some point, her exhortations got me to go before my GOD (JEHOVAH) the way my mother birthed me (naked), and I cried and prayed unto GOD – that was in 2009. In 2010, I got a job with a World Bank Project in Nasarawa state, and I left Mrs. Heidi, not because I wanted to but because I got into a rift with my supervisor.

Working with the NSCSDA was a dream; there was no international travel, but at least I was on a good salary. Unlike when I was with NBTT, I was on transport stipends, except when I travelled abroad. Mrs. Heidi wanted to arrange for me to work with her organisation, but Akilla kept the road blocked. I got another lovely woman, Aisha (a Muslim), whom I married in a traditional wedding ceremony. Aisha eventually became my colleague at work even before we married in 2014.

We had planned for the court marriage in 2015 but needed a better working relationship with the state governor. We expended our savings on daily expenses, sold our lands to pay rent, and sold our cars to get an eatery business going for Aisha; it was just a horrible experience.

In 2015, we moved into a house I had been building completed at only 50% (it was her idea). That same year, GOD so kind, I got another job with the Federal University Lafia (FULAFIA). It was a relief. We were grateful, and she jumped on me when I broke the news in a bear hug. I listened to my student enrolment advisor (Diana) that same year. I applied to the University of Roehampton, not knowing how to pay my fees – just hoping and waiting for NSCSDA to resuscitate me.

In my first year at FULAFIA, Aisha took ill. She had a miscarriage and had to go to Abuja for some tests, as recommended by her aunt. Aisha never came back home, and she died in February 2016. Quake number six, I became a drunk all over again.

The details of how I got through to this time, now married with children, living in my own house, and enjoying a joyful and prosperous life – is a divine story. Asmau, my current wife, had been married and had lost her husband in a car accident barely six months into the marriage. We found each other. I learned that a definitive test exists for leadership, often found in the crucibles of leadership, which changed my whole life and gave me a new perspective.

Like gold or silver, you will go through a fiery furnace in life, regularly being put through your tests. Raheema and Hakizimana Cara should grow to read this book because all I have done since we had them is model them according to a leadership strategy that works. By all means, I pray they will apply tact and divine wisdom to navigate and overcome life's challenges as they grow.

Asmau is currently running the Doxa House Youth Empowerment and Inclusive Development Initiative, where I am the Board Chairman. Many leaders will emerge from there someday. I hope that you, the reader, remember that to make bread, there are many processes for the flour to appear even before the bread, and always remember you are forever learning to achieve your highest potential.

CHAPTER FOUR

LEADERSHIP: THE INVISIBLE MAGNET

by Armando Licoze

"Become the type of leader that people would follow voluntarily, even if you had no title or position."
   – Brian Tracy

A famous African story tells about an account when "…a man finds an eagle chick in the mountains and forces it to live together with his chickens at home" James Aggrey (1875-1927)[1]. Eventually, the eagle flew high up in the skies. Why? Because an eagle is not a fowl but an eagle.

All leaders have a unique distinction that separates them from the crowd, not because they possess particular traits or skills but because they are unique in their leadership. They draw their leadership from their life story meaning, catalysed by the pursuit of fulfilling a vision that they are ready to sacrifice themselves to.

Leaders are faithful to their calling to lead, grounded in self-belief and value systems.

Authentic leaders excel in a community where they are open to sharing their weaknesses and allowing others to feel safe doing so. They recognise that there is no better way to lead than leading. Once, my father told me that leadership is the invisible magnet that draws people to action and holds on in the long journey. Still, I didn't understand this expression's meaning until it was tried and proven.

When I finished college in Maputo, Mozambique, I started my first employment with ADPP, a Danish charity that ran the school where I trained. A year after my employment, I accepted an invitation to further my studies in Denmark. This was one of the most exciting times in my life. "I am going to get in an airplane; I am going to Europe" was a refrain in my brain. I was responsible for leading a team of half a dozen Mozambican students.

It was clear that I had to lead this group of students to Denmark and back, ensuring they were well looked after and returned to Mozambique safely. Admittedly, this group was challenging as most students had shown interest in staying in Denmark if they could. Most of these students came from middle-class families, while I was one of three from economically disadvantaged families. I remember going to my father and asking how I had been the one to lead this team in unknown ventures. My father looked at me and gently reached to my shoulder, saying, "You were chosen because you are an eagle, once an eagle, always an eagle; that's who we are; you just need to improve your English," says he. He told me the story of the eagle and chicken; coincidentally, my surname, Licoze, means an eagle in my Xichope, my mother language. "They picked you because they saw an eagle ready for the task, not a chicken he added." I embraced the task. I travelled for the first time to neighbouring Zimbabwe, where we took our first flight to Denmark.

THE ESSENCE OF GROWTH

Leaders are at their best when they can grow from one stage to another. The critical element for growth is self-reflection and learning woven into self-confidence. Leaders are authentic when they have self-knowledge and self-concept clarity through construction, developing, and revising their life stories. Good leaders grow, develop, and learn from their mistakes to lead others effectively.

Throughout my career, I have thrived and taken pride in becoming an authentic leader. As an African proverb says: "If you want to go fast, go alone. If you want to go far, go together". This is true for leadership.

Leadership is an act to influence others for the same purpose. A leader's growth alone is not enough to fulfill the purpose of a true leader; it requires a self-reflection environment where the followers are also committed to self-learning.

When I joined Oasis in Mozambique, I realised that scaling up the organisation's operations would require me to develop an intentional learning habit as a leader. I juggled many options and decided to do my Master's degree in project management, allowing me to engage with like-minded peers and professors.

It didn't take me long to discover that self-reflection was a critical skill I had to develop. To speed up my learning, my company helped to hire an executive who assisted me in acquiring the necessary skills, which has become a practice in the organisation.

Leaders discover the way to go as they go; through self-reflection, they quickly understand their strengths and weaknesses and navigate those while focusing on the purpose of their leadership. Stages of leadership and purpose and environment require high levels of adaptation from leaders; however, the central issue is self-reflection for sustainable growth.

Leaders must know themselves better to build confidence and draw others to join. When I took the mission to scale up the organisation, I knew something was missing, and I had to go and find it. No one size fits all, but all leaders know when that thing is missing and find ways to get it.

Authentic leaders rely on experiential learning for their development, and there is no one set school for them as they develop from self-relevant meaning. Authentic leaders are like ordinary people trying to learn a new skill, drawing from past experiences and knowledge intrinsically embedded in life's purposes.

These individuals are recognisable for their commitment and loyalty to an organisation, regardless of rank or status. I am in my early 50s, but whenever I find my childhood friends or former colleagues, I observe that very few are still committed to what they believed then.

Still, the majority have moved on but talk about their frustration at not being able to do any fulfilling job, and I always ask, do you want to talk about it. The response is always yes with a broken heart and "Wake it up; it's waiting." You can only develop what is there. If you cannot find it, you cannot make it.

A social development expert, a friend of mine, Raj Joseph, once said that "those who don't believe that people can develop themselves are in the wrong business; this is a business for those who consider everyone in the community can change for good".

In my 30 years of experience in community transformation across slums in Africa, Asia, and Europe, I have witnessed many stories of change from real people with amazing families whose stories have transformed them. People can respond to their own stories if there is someone to love and stimulate that inner connection.

Throughout my career, people believed in me. They entrusted me with more responsibility not because I was the best but because they believed in me and stimulated my development, which has played a critical role in my life story and leadership.

I witnessed colleagues with whom I participated in their development rising to senior positions in the organisation and others taking senior roles in international organisations. It shows that those who are willing need someone to stimulate their desires to grow to reach their potential.

BEING RESILIENT

"During my lifetime, I have dedicated myself to this struggle of the African people. I have fought against white domination, and I have fought against black domination. I have cherished the ideal of a democratic and free society in which all persons live together in harmony and with equal opportunities. It is an ideal that I hope to live for and to achieve. But if needs be, it is an ideal for which I am prepared to die." – Nelson Mandela.

This speech was one of the best speeches of the last century, beyond Nelson Mandela, but of a vision for a free society for which he was ready to die. Nelson Mandela's leadership was applauded by all those who joined him in the struggle to be free from an authoritarian society, which sometimes caused controversy in the black community that wanted to seek revenge for white domination. He fought against white and black supremacy for an ideal transcending skin colour, an equal society for all.

Nelson Mandela spent one-third of his life in prison on a mission to liberate South Africa from Apartheid, and only the story of success kept him ener- gised in the dark moments of the struggle. He refused to compromise his commitment to his fight to trade with his freedom.

When it seems impossible, true leaders rely on the big story that resonates with them and helps them energise others to press on till the end. Albert Einstein once said, "Logic will take you from A to B; imagination will take you everywhere." This applies to authentic leaders. They know that most stories of brevity are done in the community, celebrated by the community, and replicated in that community, hence the mobilization of others to join in leadership.

To be resilient, one must be able to recover quickly from difficulties. Bouncing back can be challenging when a leader is motivated by status or money or any quick gratification, but for those who carry in themselves a vision and a mission, the process of bouncing back is energising, and they recognise that their comeback is stronger.

It always seems impossible till it's done, says Mandela. Leaders have an arduous task, and they deal with multiple uncertainties in their daily journey as they draw others to see what is at the other end to challenge them to trust and follow. The end story that others cannot see is what energises them.

Resilient leaders are ready to adapt. Leaders must be able to use all at their disposal to fulfill the mission. If a leader was a rock player, they should be able to play Jazz if required.

When the African National Congress (ANC) was banned in South Africa, Mandela considered armed struggle the only viable option. Later, he was granted permission to start the ANC military wing Umkhonto we Sizwe, an underground military movement engaged in sabotage, which led to his life imprisonment, accused of high treason and conspiracy against the state. The motivation for Mandela was to win against apartheid.

Intrinsically, resilient leaders recognise that leading can be daunting and chilling cold in uncertain moments. Resilience defines leaders who persevere and come out stronger against all odds, just like Nelson Mandela, who overcame to become the first black president of South Africa and led the country in the pursuit of unity.

When South Africa hosted the 1995 Rugby World Cup, Mandela cheered the team for an imaginable victory. He was confident and believed in being victorious, and because of this, he mobilised black and white people to stand together for the nation beyond racial differences, and they won. The World Cup Rugby was one of Nelson Mandela's tools to fulfill his commitment to a free society.

CHAPTER FIVE

FUNCTIONING EFFECTIVELY IN CRISIS

by Ann Austin

I had to accept responsibility even if I hadn't asked for it. As the oldest of nine children, I adore my seven younger brothers and sister. I remember growing up and caring for my siblings when my parents had to go to work while we were on vacation from school or on weekends when they had to attend an event. In those moments, I would play the role of a mother, or "Ada," as the first daughter, widely known in Nigeria's Igbo tribe.

My mother would often remind me that I was her first fruit and that God had brought me as the first child for a reason, so taking on the role of a leader was a natural part of my existence. "God does not make mistakes; he brought you first for a reason. *"Be a good example and a leader to your siblings; they are watching and learning from you," she* frequently advises.

My parents had left me with my immediate younger sister on this particular day. They were only going to a function and would return soon. However, the clock was ticking, and we could soon hear the crickets outside the window, beckoning the arrival of nightfall.

I looked at my sister, who was yawning while trying to stay awake, anticipating the special treats that often accompanied our parents on their outings. But this day was different. First, I had to ensure that my siblings had eaten, and I realised how difficult it must have been for my mother when we all refused to eat or craved something else after she cooked.

At that moment, I had to admit that decision-making is one of the most challenging things a leader can do, and my mother makes decisions daily, but it was my turn. So, I asked my brothers and sister, and we all agreed to cook yam. Everything was fine until I began to dance, but it was not a dance of joy that I had succeeded in cooking a delicious meal, but a dance of itchiness.

The fluid from the yam peels, called calcium oxalate saponins, itches the skin when it touches it. Because I was in charge and didn't want to scare my sister, who was now staring at me with perplexity, I couldn't panic. So, what do you do? I recalled that my mother had mentioned using palm oil to relieve the itching caused by yam peels. Fortunately, she was always prepared and kept materials like this on hand, and thank God, it worked.

After dining, we returned to the sitting room, where a candle was gently burning on the table and emitting a nice glow. The girls were getting bored, so I had to keep them occupied. I then started telling a story. My uncle told me a tale about the lowly princess when we were under his care. I wasn't aware that my sister was getting close to the flame while I narrated the story.

Everything started with a stench of burning rubber, and when I glanced over, her hair was already on fire! She was sobbing, and my other sister screamed in fear, "Fire! Help! Is she going to die?" At that moment, so many questions flashed before me. What would I do? My parents had left them in my care.

What justifications would I have offered the neighbours if something serious occurred? I needed to think quickly. I had to act and take responsibility, but I couldn't scream or cry because it would have made the poor girl even more anxious. I recalled the big bowls of water put away in our storage room earlier that day and immediately took her in my arms, dashing to the store to quench the fire.

Upon their return, my parents were visibly shocked but expressed relief that nothing serious had occurred to my sister, and I shared their comfort. I considered the circumstance and asked myself: What would I have done if my Mum had not stocked the ingredients earlier? Or if we hadn't stored bowls of water earlier that day? What if the fire worsened because I panicked, cried for a long time, or possibly even froze in shock?

Over the years, I've understood that great leaders can handle challenging circumstances even when they don't have all the solutions. Giving yourself a title or a position is simple, but the real test is if you can lead others, accept responsibility, and be resilient in the face of obstacles.

Every leader must exhibit resilience because it demonstrates your capacity for navigating a world where others depend on you. Life is never simple, and the road is never straight.

PREPAREDNESS DOESN'T STOP AT PLAN B

How About D, E, or Even F?

What do you know, and how can it help you in unexpected situations? A true leader always approaches a problem with an open vessel. You anticipate challenges half of the time, even when you don't? How do you intend to resolve it? Having a backup and another backup plan is a principle I have adopted in my life values and career thus far, especially when I want something to work.

I once heard that having a plan B keeps you from focusing on your plan A, but that's not entirely true. It is not because you should not put your best effort into your initial plan that you develop a plan B, C, or more. In fact, as a leader, you are expected always to give your all. However, what if your best wasn't good enough the first time, or if that strategy needed to be tweaked or re-tweaked to work?

Disappointments and unanticipated occurrences will inevitably occur, and when they do, we frequently feel lost and confused. However, if you plan for such circumstances and create a backup strategy, you are more likely to feel safe knowing that you have other options.

Think about how many tries it took Thomas Edison, one of the greatest inventors in American history, to create the light bulb. He tried various methods and was unsuccessful, yet he never gave up. He tried multiple strategies to accomplish his goals after each setback until he eventually saw the light. Plan B is when we must revise our plan due to uncontrollable circumstances.

Having a backup plan does not imply a lack of assurance or commitment to your goals. But what if Plan B doesn't work or doesn't produce the expected results? As a leader, you are relentless and committed to achieving your objectives, even if that means implementing D, E, or F plans until you solve the problem or get it right. Backup plans are essential because they prepare you for uncertainty and disappointments and effectively respond when they occur.

Plans D, E, or F serve to decrease the likelihood of failure and its effects. Backup plans make you more robust, calm, and self-assured since you know you always have a plan, improving your agility as a leader in unforeseen circumstances.

TAKING RESPONSIBILITY

Many believe that fleeing a situation or placing blame is the easier option. But as a leader, you cannot hurl accusations around in the heat of the moment or attempt to run away or avoid the problem. I've discovered that when you opt for either, you frequently worsen the situation as you see it turn into a mountain before your eyes or show that you are unfit to occupy the leadership role entrusted to you.

A few months ago, as part of my routine as an editor, I was reading through my emails and reviewing submissions when I came across this horrifying email. I was perplexed when I opened it because it said, "Copyright Infringement Notification," even though I'm usually cautious. How on earth could I have missed this, given that I repeatedly warned the writers I worked with about the consequences of copyright violations?

I had to call an urgent meeting with my entire staff working remotely. I spoke with the author who had put us in that predicament one-on-one and questioned why she hadn't credited the image's creator. She explained that because the image had been in circulation for a while, it had been difficult to determine its trustworthy source, and she didn't want to give credit to the wrong person.

It was the first time we found ourselves in such a situation that could cost our startup company money and land us in a lawsuit if we weren't careful, and yes, I was concerned.

Even though the writer had made a rookie mistake that put us at risk of losing money, I understood her point of view and refused to blame her for it. I also had to hold myself accountable because it was my responsibility as an editor to check before publication. So, I set up a meeting with the writers and re-educated them on the subject while providing more resources to assist them in doing better as I attempted to calm the situation with our legal team. In essence, you must be able to handle situations with maturity and professionalism to be a leader.

When leaders constantly accept responsibility for their actions, they demonstrate their dependability in trying situations and ability to scale through tough times. Instead of avoiding accountability, a good leader solves a problem. Rather than assigning blame, they accept responsibility for the issue and work to resolve it. Remember that everyone makes mistakes now and again, and leaders are no different. But good leaders understand that it is better to speak of blunders in terms of "we" and take responsibility for their group. Failure-related scenarios or mishaps won't frighten them; they'll stand by their team when things become challenging.

YOU DON'T KNOW IT ALL

Since I started writing this chapter, "Unexpected Events" has been a recurring theme. Most of the time, we don't prepare for a crisis; instead, it's more like unanticipated bugs trying to infiltrate a project or business that might be succeeding. You don't pray for a problem to arise, but sometimes you have to figure out what to do when it does, on the spot, at that very moment.

As a leader, it is easy to carry the burden entirely on your shoulders. You should demonstrate that you can handle a crisis independently and avoid appearing weak. We often fail to comprehend that refusing to admit our fragility or seek aid is a sign of weakness. You just cannot be all-knowing. You possess only some of the solutions.

The strongest leaders understand that success depends on working as a team. Asking for help demonstrates strength rather than weakness. Indeed, "two heads are better than one", and I've come to believe this is true when exploring ideas as a leader.

Your team might find it comforting to know you are open to recommendations. At the same time, you work to find answers to an issue, and showing your humanity could improve the corporate culture. You should know that displaying vulnerability is not the same as expressing fear.

It would help if you were strong, maybe not for you, but for others.

A leader takes charge and quells the escalating hysteria. When word of a crisis spreads, this is frequently the first thing a leader must do. There is a cost to leadership. It would help if you determined whether you are willing to pay the price. Are you prepared to put others' needs ahead of your own? Authentic leadership entails doing things like this during uncertainty for your team.

A good leader can address issues head-on, even when there is no immediate way out. Who will look for a solution if you panic, your supporters panic, and everyone else panics? Nobody. Being calm in the moment and repeatedly telling myself that everything will be fine helps me even when I'm at a loss for what to do. After all, don't cry over spilled milk and blame SELF or others, but instead try to clean up the mess and possibly get better jars. you will see, there will always be a light at the end of the tunnel.

CHAPTER SIX

"Bring happiness wherever you go, not whenever you go." - Oscar Wilde

THE QUALITY OF JOY

by Gary Chandler

I get rather tired of reading yet another leadership definition by a self-proclaimed guru who has finally found the Holy Grail of all things "leaderish." Why are we seemingly on an endless quest to discover the perfect leadership secrets? Over the years, literature has been replete with varying leadership descriptions such as transformational, transactional, authentic, servant, ethical, visionary, etc.

All these descriptors have thousands of "fine" words describing their attributes. But I have a request – let's not mention the "L-word" in this chapter too often. Instead, let us consider the admirable qualities we are trying to discover. In other words, what makes anyone want to follow another person, initially? There is one rarely mentioned quality that certainly grabs my attention: joy. Returning to Mr. Wilde's quote on happiness, I would prefer to replace "happiness" with "joy." Why?

Happiness generally occurs in a moment; it is fleeting and circumstance based.

On the other hand, "joy" is built into our very core. It is not temporary and does not depend on changing circumstances. It is a perpetual state without necessarily requiring happiness all the time. Joy transcends circumstances and spreads to bring out the best in humankind. It can be a choice.

As a parallel for choosing joy over happiness, Viktor Frankl describes his attitude while imprisoned in a Nazi concentration camp, **"The one thing you cannot take away from me is how I choose to respond to what you do to me. The last of one's freedoms is to choose one's attitude in any given circumstance."**[1] His wisdom here continues to inspire us today. Then why does choosing joy attract followers and consequently help create a leader?

Let's get personal. Try to remember who has brought the most joy into your life. Is it a specific family member, a friend, a co-worker, or a casual acquaintance? Or is it someone you've noticed from a distance, watching them closely and how they interact with others? Perhaps someone who has a spiritual relationship brings them incomprehensible peace.

Whomever it may be, think deeply and intently about this person. Why does this particular relationship bring a smile to your face? What is it about this person that appeals to you despite circumstances? Or, if you haven't experienced such a person yet, how might you describe a joyful person, and what impact might they need to transfer that joy to you?

These are questions that I often ask my younger self. Some lucky people are born into a life with positive role models to admire. Others, like me, learn how to influence people through adversity. I sought someone who emulated the kind of man I hoped to be. I didn't understand what I desired because I'd not yet witnessed it.

GROWING UP

Growing up in the south of England, joy was not part of my life. My family often struggled to make ends meet, and there were many times when I felt unsafe since we lived in a rough neighborhood. My father was away quite a bit and didn't spend time with my three younger siblings and me when he was home. The pub and his friends were his home away from home. I think he was forced to take on the responsibility of being a father far too early and, unfortunately, took out many of his frustrations on my mother.

Forged in anger, aggression, and dishonesty are the qualities I learned from him. I remember getting into many fights in and after school, perhaps due to frustration or just because I could fight. Or maybe it was because I had to appear tough to navigate through my younger childhood environment. Sadly, I certainly picked up some undesirable character traits.

For instance, I also remember stealing sweets from the local sweetshop, except on Sundays. On this holy day, my parents would send the four of us by ourselves to church with 10 pence each for the collection plate. Naturally, we spent the money at the same sweet shop instead, and the donation never reached the plate. We got to know the proprietor quite well. At other times, my friend Billy and I would walk to the seaside fun fair for the afternoon even though we had no money to spend.

Occasionally, I would convince him to rifle through his mom's handbag and find some change. We had fun, so I didn't feel bad for Billy at the time, although now I wonder how often this eroded his parents' trust in him.

It pains me to say I followed in the wrong footsteps back then. I did not have a positive male role model to emulate while growing up; I wish I had. Yet I knew, even at that young age, the kind of man I did not want to become. And so, my childhood progressed into my teen years, and I began to turn away from unfavourable qualities. My search for a better way continued.

When I was almost thirteen, my family emigrated to Canada. It was the best decision my parents had ever made, ever. Looking back, I understand we might have had to leave as my Dad repeatedly got into trouble with the law. It may have been his only option. We initially lived in the Toronto area near my mother's two brothers, who had emigrated a few years earlier. After three years, we moved further west to Vancouver, where the weather was more like that in the U.K. The Toronto winters and oppressive summer heat were a little too extreme.

We moved around the Vancouver area several times for the first six years, wherever we could find the best rental. My Dad would still be gone for periods, mostly on weekends. It is sad to say, but he continued the same dishonest behavior he displayed in the U.K. My Mom kept most of this hidden from my siblings and me and always put on a brave face.

Looking back on this period, I realise that she lived with many repulsive spousal behaviours from my Dad to keep the family together for the sake of her children. I am forever in her debt. However, I still had not met anyone I wanted to be and behave like. Life was a problem: no one I knew had a spirit of joy. My teenage challenges pointed me toward adult ambitions. I needed to find a better way, but how?

After graduating from high school, I decided to pursue a career as a pilot. It was a big dream for a kid like me, but, as a twelve-year-old on my first flight, I remember sitting by the window in the 747 aircraft as we flew across the Atlantic, thinking to myself, 'One day, I'm going to fly this.' Somehow, my parents scraped enough money to send me to aviation college, even though this three-year program was expensive. After hard work and persistence, I graduated with a commercial pilot's license and a multi-engine rating. It was the first meaningful accomplishment of my life, and it gave me confidence.

AIR FORCE DAYS AND MARRIAGE WAYS

I met the love of my life when I was 22. On our third date, I confidently told Leslie I would marry her someday. Well, it didn't quite scare her off, but looking back, maybe it was a little too presumptuous. Even though I had already decided, she had other plans: to graduate from university (which she did), find a good teaching job, and then move into her own place. Maybe then she would be ready to get married. But, of course, I came along and threw a wrench into her plans.

At first, her steadfastness towards her goal caused me to propose to her on three occasions over an 18-month timeframe! Third time lucky, I guess. Leslie has been my bedrock ever since, and even now, as I write thirty-eight years later, the thought of her strength, joy, and beauty still brings tears to my eyes. My elusive search to find a spirit of joy was starting to materialise.

I searched for a flying position during our courtship, but the economy did not allow it. Instead, I worked at several jobs, including my Dad's construction company. From him, I learned a practical and beneficial skillset, and it has been an asset to my family and me even to this day.

One day, out of the blue, my Dad introduced the thought that I should join the Royal Canadian Air Force. It hadn't even occurred to me! Yet, I applied and was extremely excited to be accepted into Officer Training. Here, I learned about real teamwork and leadership for the first time. We often had several tasks to complete as leaders and followers. I understood that for one to succeed, we all had to rely on the team to cross the finish line together. In these scenarios, arrogance and dishonesty were the enemies of accomplishment. This new way of approaching life's challenges appealed to me greatly.

After three months of intense leadership training, I had forged friendships with those I had grown to admire and began to realise that integrity was an invaluable asset. I graduated from Officer Training and went on to Flight Training. What followed was a demanding and stressful two-year period. The difference between washing out and succeeding was razor-edged thin. One could fail two flight tests during the jet training phase, but a third meant termination.

To add to my challenges, I also had another new distraction: my wife's pregnancy. Although extremely exciting, it was also nerve-wracking as I had to graduate to provide for my new family, yet I had already failed two flight tests. Leslie helped me to memorise emergency procedures and checklist items night after night, as I needed help to prevent another failure. My rock of a wife probably learned the techniques better than I did. No matter the task, all members of my training squadron would always encourage and help anyone who needed it, and I benefitted immensely from this support. Eventually, I white-knuckled this test successfully, made it through, and earned my Wings. It was an intensely gratifying moment in my life.

My parents attended the Wings presentation, and both were incredibly proud. Although I would not describe these two years of stressful training as joyful, it taught me that the power a team, a squadron or a husband and wife, can develop when striving to achieve a common objective together.

The years flew by, literally. I spent my career in the RCAF, flying the C-130 Hercules transport aircraft, the CT-134 Musketeer ab initio training aircraft, and the C-90A multi-engine trainer. I embraced this adventurous lifestyle when visiting 37 countries and circumnavigating the globe twice. As an Aircraft Commander, I felt privileged to lead people twice my age and learned much about what not to do.

For a twenty-seven-year-old Aircraft Commander to be able to lead 30 to 50-year-olds around the world, humility is required by the bucketload, as well as never-ending respect for the professionalism and integrity of others and trust in the entire crew to complete each mission effectively. I made more friends than ever before. The camaraderie I experienced in the military has never been matched since. I had a happy home with two wonderful children. For the first time, I felt on top of my game. I began to taste what joy could be like...when things were going well.

Personal circumstances dictated the time for my departure from the RCAF. My wife's father was diagnosed with a terminal illness, so we moved west to be closer to her parents. The previous ten years had equipped me with confidence in my skills and abilities and a supportive wife, so I believed I was ready for change and began examining other career prospects. I was enamoured by the financial success that the eldest of my two younger brothers seemed to enjoy on Canada's West Coast. The "grass is always greener" syndrome captured me.

I never considered myself materialistic before this point, but his apparent monetary and material success perhaps stirred something profound in me that I had been suppressing. I lost sight of what I had learned to date and decided to measure my own "success" on a financial scale. It was a path down a different route, and thus, it was that I began to follow someone for the wrong reasons.

THE DARKEST HOUR

My brother had become a land developer and offered me a contract position with his company. Since I was seeking employment in the civilian world for the first time in 10 years, he made me an offer too good to refuse. I believed him when he told me it would provide me with immediate income to support my family and the potential of a good commission.

My job was to raise private capital to fund land acquisitions that his company would develop and build. I was pretty successful for the first eighteen months since I tapped into my previous military network for clients. At his urging, I also invested all my military severance pay in showing my investors how much I trusted my brother and his company.

Since we had built a well-established friendship and camaraderie over the past decade, my RCAF friends were happy to invest with the hopes of an above-average rate of return. It was a win-win. I would send them monthly dividend cheques and newsletters informing them of the developments' progress. I met with my brother once a week for updates, and for a while, everything seemed great. All our clients were happy.

UNTIL THINGS CHANGED

Occasionally, interest cheques began to miss their due date. I conferred with my brother, and he artfully explained that this was just the nature of land developments, the ebb and flow of cash, as it were. I dutifully passed this news to my investors. Most understood. Then, the payments became even more sporadic. As good friends invested so much, I grew more concerned, yet my brother assuaged my worries with believable, smooth-talking, and confidence. So, again, I passed along his information to the investors, including my wife. Soon, the lack of repayments became too frequent to excuse. I began to worry that this was not "just normal."

One fateful morning, I met my brother for a serious one-to-one conversation over coffee. The discussion grew somewhat heated, so we decided to cool down before continuing the talk privately. We both agreed to meet early the next day at his home.

I arrived at his house at 8a.m. the following day as planned. The shock that greeted me is something I will never forget. The front door was wide open, and the house was vacant. He and his family were gone, vanished without a trace! Not a speck of furniture or hint that anyone had ever lived there.

My heart raced. It felt like the ground gave way under my feet. I lost my breath and felt like passing out. On my ten-minute drive back to my house, I went through all the possible scenarios of why he wasn't there. Then it hit me: it had all been an unthinkable betrayal.

My thoughts swirled: what to say to our investors, my good friends, and even more recent clients! Had we been scammed, I wondered, "What do I do now?" My brother owed about $2,000,000 back to the investors! Some had mortgaged their homes, taken out loans, or used their life savings. Even my wife's aging parents had re-mortgaged their house to invest, not to mention our investments. To a person, they had all trusted me – and I had trusted my brother. How could I expect others to think I was betrayed if I had difficulty believing this?

THUS BEGAN THE DARKEST PERIOD OF MY LIFE

My friends who had invested abandoned me. All of them. How could I blame them? They automatically assumed I was part of this "scam" since my brother was my brother. Before long, the Royal Canadian Mounted Police (RCMP) Commercial Crime Division began investigating me. I had lawsuit after lawsuit filed against me. Several vendors came after me for payment, even knocking violently on our front door with my family, frightened inside.

Unbeknownst to me, my brother had forged my signature and somehow fraudulently obtained my social insurance number, opening various accounts with construction suppliers. He had even rented an apartment in my name!

Unpaid phone bills — his, not "mine", sent to my address in my name.

I received the police summons for unpaid parking and speeding tickets, which my brother had accumulated while posing as me. I also received a payment request for a Mercedes he had leased in my name. Things were unravelling fast, and I was going downhill even more quickly. Pandora's Box was wide open. My whole world was suddenly falling apart!

I began to live in a perpetual zombie zone, not knowing if I was coming or going. Before long, I succumbed to a nervous breakdown. I probably wouldn't be around today if it weren't for my wife's steadfastness and belief in me. Leslie always maintained that she knew I was still the man of integrity she had married. We quickly had no choice but to declare bankruptcy. Our cars and computers were repossessed.

We could not pay rent and had to move in with my mother-in-law. I was under a doctor's care and was prescribed anti-depressants. I think they helped and reduced my suicidal thoughts, which was a tremendous relief to my wife. I can't see how I would have committed suicide: it just is not in my make-up to give up, but the medication was an insurance policy my wife was keen to make.

I couldn't sleep through the night: I woke up at 3a.m. every morning, soaking wet with sweat and shaking violently. In the middle of every night, my wife would have to change our sheets and calm me down, which went on for about three months. I remember being down to our last $20. I can still picture my beautiful wife rifling through the couch cushions, looking for change to buy milk for our two young children. It was tough to keep the kids insulated from what was going on. They were merely 7 and 8 years old but sensed something unpleasant was happening around them. We did all we could to mask our nightmare's reality from our two young children, yet they were perceptive.

Soon, our son began having difficulties at school. My wife and I felt alone together. At the time, most of my family didn't understand that any family member could have done to another what my brother did to me (yet in time, they did). It was utterly incomprehensible. Nevertheless, my wife and I never waivered as a couple.

Leslie carried an enormous load, protecting our children, monitoring our daily situation, encouraging me, and managing the legal shenanigans. All this while her father was nearing the end of his life. I will forever be in her debt. Her empathy, encouragement, and trust that I would get through this all and eventually provide for our family again were always evident.

THE TURNING POINT

We had never been overtly spiritual: Leslie had a Catholic upbringing but had drifted from her faith. I was only a Christmas and Easter attendee at the local Anglican church when growing up. But timing is everything. At our lowest point, a local pastor knocked on our door to get his Good News message to his neighbours. My wife opened the door and abruptly closed it after a brief exchange. However, had a seed of hope been planted? We had never considered attending attending church as a respite from what was happening to and around us. Faith didn't appear in our uncharted options as a rescue destination. Soon afterward, though, I uncharacteristically proclaimed, "Let's go to church this morning." The look of astonishment from three pairs of eyes upon hearing such an announcement was comical. "Church?"

As we no longer had a car, we walked to the closest church we could find, a Baptist church, not that I knew the difference in any of the many denominations. I thought a church was a church. However, we went in. Believe it or not, the pastor was the same one on whom my wife had closed the door. Luckily, I don't think he recognised us amongst the other 200 congregants. We were welcomed at the door and sat down. And then, I experienced something completely unexpected that forever changed my life.

The songs began, not traditional hymns as I expected, but contemporary Christian music and lyrics. The lyrics seemed to speak directly to me, no one else (well, of course, they did, but that is what it felt like to me). Words of hope, faith, joy, love, and encouragement sprung into the mind and heart of someone yearning for a way out.

I started sobbing like an idiot in front of 200 strangers. Then, suddenly, a wave of hot energy coursed through my body. It entered my head and left through my fingertips. I was frightened. Yet, it was calming and loving. To this day, it isn't easy to explain. But it was so real and, as far as I knew, unique to me.

On the walk home, my wife noticed something quite different about me and looked at me warily. A peaceful presence emanated from me, and she saw me smiling for the first time in many months. I was still too confused to understand what had happened, but I felt at peace despite my circumstances. That night, I slept right through the night for the first time in months. I could have slept longer, but Leslie shook me awake at 7a.m. for fear that I had finally kicked the bucket!

A few weeks later, after seeing that my inexplicable peace was not fading into memory, she also decided to follow me on this new path. We had both found something worth living for, a peace that surpasses understanding. We had found joy!

From then on, we were calmer and felt like we had finally found solid ground. Our painful legal and financial issues still had to be dealt with, and they did not miraculously disappear, but I was able to bring a focus and resonance to the tasks at hand that I couldn't do before.

When we invited the pastor back to our house a few weeks later, he explained what had happened, and we prayed together (twenty-five years later, although separated by thousands of kilometres, we are still excellent friends). Amazing and unexpectedly positive things began to happen. For example, we met a fellow online, and he encouraged us in our newfound faith. Later, we discovered that he and his family lived only about 40 minutes south of us in Lynden, Washington. Thus began a new friendship that is still going on today even though we are still separated by several thousand kilometres.

But back then, we would go across the Canada-US border to visit with our new friends. We often came home unaware that several hundred dollars had been hidden in our car or my wife's purse and armed with a few delicious homemade pies. Years later, we learned several churches in Lynden were raising this money through a series of garage sales they had hosted just for us! How amazed we were at the time that these unexpected funds kept "magically" appearing, visit after visit! Indeed, my humble milkman friend loaned us his pick-up truck for three months while we were scraping together enough money for our vehicle.

For three months, he and his family used his milk delivery truck as their only transportation. Such selflessness I had never experienced. I admired these people, and I wanted to be more like them! Our new friend helped me to redefine what I wanted out of life. In Larry Julian's book, "God is My CEO", he states, "Success is generally defined as an outcome, whereas significance concerns the process."[2] My former life's circumstances forced me to reevaluate my direction in life. I decided to lead a life of significance over success. Tangible outcomes derived from success are still required but not paramount overall. However, living a life of significance allows one to make a positive impact or difference on all those around you, family, and work colleagues.

In his book, "The Fred Factor," Mark Sanborn discusses significance by stating, "One thing seems common for all human beings: a passion for significance. Everyone wants to count, to know that what they do each day isn't simply a way of making a living, but a living of making meaning.'[3] So, my path to significance began. However, I still believed that my 'process' must focus on my family. My "significance journey" should be about impacting them first. A man does what he must do to support his family.

I found a humble but honest job packing books for a Christian warehouse. It was a welcome distraction from the ongoing issues, and I felt blessed to be able to work again. Since we still had no car, my pastor sold us his old car for a dollar! Once again, we were recipients of unbelievable kindness! It was a reverse convertible: the floor was open, but the roof was not. We had to be careful not to put our feet on the floor as we might have lost them through the gaping hole under the gas pedal! We laughed about our new Flintstone mobile! However, we could now return our friend's truck, and this car allowed my wife to drive to her new teaching job.

Things were slowly starting to turn around from a legal perspective as well. After a year of investigation, eventually, I was cleared by the RCMP of any wrongdoing. Because of our bankruptcy and my brother's fraud committed against us, all the vendors gradually withdrew their claims for payment. Leslie began picking up teaching jobs, and the income was greatly appreciated. The road we found ourselves on wasn't easy, but we saw it was leading us in the right direction.

We had other encouragement from entirely unexpected sources. Late one stressful morning, Leslie was returning from delivering court documents and experienced a direct word from God. As she was momentarily paused in traffic, she felt a powerful sensation of love charged throughout her body, and she audibly heard the words, 'Gary will be ok.' She knew, directly from God, that if Gary were okay, then the entire family would be OK. She pulled over and wept. It was her experience, and nobody can refute it. It gave her the peace and joy of knowing that God is "real", and everything will be fine.

Earlier, I wrote that joy was the ultimate state in so many words. When you understand and believe things will work out (but not always how you plan them to), this deep-seated confidence inspires others to trust you as an authentic person and potential leader. Bringing joy wherever you go infuses all those around you to view everything with a more positive perspective.

Even when circumstances are challenging, tapping into your profound joy will put all those around you at ease. However, being authentically joyful doesn't mean wearing a fake smile or putting on a "joy cape" when only at work. It means being assured and confidently at peace in your core, 24/7. Although not explicitly alluding to joy, John Maxwell's book '**Developing the Leader Within You'** mentions that integrity is something you own in yourselves before leading others. [4]

Joy comes from knowing that something bigger than yourself is at play, something that you may not understand but has your eternal life as its focus. Nothing can destroy it. It can be shaken since we are all human, but it never fails. Once you have found the source of true joy, it can never be taken away without your permission. Experiencing life with joy also allows us to be vulnerable to healing. And to heal, we need another quality.

It's not an easy journey, to get to a place where you forgive people. But it is such a powerful place because it frees you.
 - Tyler Perry

FORGIVENESS

As human beings, genuine forgiveness is something that we all find challenging, especially when we have been hurt to the core. Nevertheless, to be genuinely joyful, we must release the bitterness of the past and not allow its poison to affect us moving forward.

Withholding forgiveness doesn't hurt the aggressor; it only negatively impacts the wounded. It festers and affects all those around and close to you. At times, its toxic head appears suddenly, perhaps in the heat of a discussion with a loved one or colleague. Maybe one does not even realise that this unforgiveness is at the root of the outburst, but most times, it is. Leaders cannot be authentic and joyful leaders if they harbour unforgiveness in their hearts.

Two years after my brother infamously disappeared, I finally discovered he had left Canada and later moved to Phoenix, Arizona. He and his family were victims of a drunk driver and were grievously injured. My brother suffered a broken back, and my nephew had a seriously fractured thigh bone. I knew I had to forgive him. I had no choice but to do so. I could not let what he did to me and my family fester for 50-plus years and possibly have devastating impacts through my behaviour on my wife, children, and grandchildren. I had to break this cycle.

As a Christian, I must be willing to forgive others regardless of their trespasses against me, so I flew down to Phoenix and visited my brother in the hospital. Fortunately, his back would heal, although he had to spend the next two weeks recovering in care. When I entered his room, he was pretty surprised to see me.

I suppose he didn't think I knew where to find him. I didn't want to stay long, so I walked up to his bed, kissed him on the forehead, and told him, "I forgive you." He looked at me and coldly said, "It was only business." As I briefly looked at him, it struck me that, sadly, not only did he break his back, but he was also a broken man. At this point, it was clear that I could not fix him. Yet, I had accomplished what I had planned to do, so I left. The funny thing about forgiveness is that even though you genuinely and sincerely forgive someone, which I did, the need in one's head and heart is to forgive that person repeatedly.

The bitterness or hurt can be so profound that, although, it is tough to forgive, once doesn't seem enough. So, I occasionally remind myself that I have forgiven him. Over the years, I've grown to understand that my brother is a sociopath, and there is no cure for him other than divine intervention. I pray for this. As I write, he has been described by an American judge as a "financial predator." He currently serves six years in a California prison for fraud, unrelated to his dealings with me.

Thankfully, it is rare to cross paths with a sociopath, but I have learned that I cannot be an honest leader if I harbour bitterness. This barrier prevents you from putting yourself into other people's shoes and being empathetic. If you are bitter, you will always be focusing on yourself, no matter how you may think you're not. Bitterness must be dealt with if you wish to be an empowering leader who pushes others to reach their full potential and become role models. Deal with anger and resentment through forgiveness, whether to yourself, your spouse, another family member, a colleague, a teacher, or any other influential person. You must deal with it to become a truly authentic leader. When you do, others will notice. That new-found peace you have through forgiveness will germinate over time into joy. When you enter a room, others will see an aura of calm despite your circumstances and gravitate toward you.

People will ask for your advice and input because your innate joy will put them at ease. Joy doesn't mean coming to work full of laughter and bubbles. It simply means that because you have erased all bitterness and unforgiveness in your heart, you can actively listen, encourage, and develop potential in others because you are no longer concerned with yourself. Not being concerned with yourself evolves into humility. Being humble opens the gateway to vulnerability and eventually leads to trust, which is the goal of everyone working together for a greater purpose.

How can one demonstrate genuine humility if harbouring bitterness and re-sentment? Here again, validating that forgiveness is the key to unequivocally showing vulnerability and developing a personal integrity worthy of trust. If you have a family, they are your primary concern, period. Children growing up notice bitterness and resentment like a canary in a coal mine. They are your primary responsibility. Develop your sense of peace and joy with them first and foremost. Talk to them about forgiving others. Let them see you and your spouse reconciling in the right way. Set the example, then take it to work. Live it. Be authentic.

PICKING UP THE PIECES

When we were slowly picking up the pieces, my other brother, the "good" one, offered me a position as a business manager for his wife's family business. It was a terrific opportunity and a rather large pay increase from working in a book warehouse. I will always be grateful to him and his wife's family. We were finally getting back on our feet. My wife was offered a full-time teaching position at a private school, and our two kids could attend the same school for free. We were so grateful!

Then, after four years, it was time to move once again. I heard through the grapevine that Nav Canada was hiring. I applied and, to my surprise (as I had been away from aviation for six years), was offered a position. However, this job meant moving from British Columbia to Ottawa, a six-day drive. After ten years in the RCAF, my wife was thrilled to be closer to her family finally. But we knew this move would align perfectly with our plans, so we said our tearful goodbyes to family and friends and embarked on the next stage of our journey together.

When we left for Ontario, my wife humorously said that you can only see two things clearly from outer space: The Great Wall of China and her heel marks across the prairies. Yet, even though our lives were back on the right path, we still had challenges to overcome in our new province. Being bankrupt made us unable to qualify for a mortgage once we arrived in Ottawa. It was a somewhat desperate situation, so we prayed for a solution.

A fellow who also began working at Nav Canada the same day as I did, whom I had only known for three months, listened to my story, and despite it and to my utter astonishment, he and his wife offered to co-sign for our mortgage. How incredible that somebody I had known for three months would put their family at financial risk for an acquaintance. We had a common faith bond and recognised where this selflessness originated. Again, we were blessed. I thoroughly enjoyed my 20 years at Nav Canada. After the first four years, I joined the ranks of management. I was privileged to lead several small teams over the years and developed a close relationship with my team members.

Often, I am asked, who were your mentors? Who did you look up to, or who was your best leader? Owing to the management framework at the time, I have yet to personally report to a superior who entirely fits that description, with perhaps one notable exception. Many leaders were in positions of authority because of their technical knowledge and not due to their people skills; others, because of close relationships and nepotism.

My second-to-last boss, however, was the closest I have come to experiencing joyful leadership. Whenever a team member entered her office, she had a smile waiting for them. She was always open but direct and particularly good at active listening. At one off-site team-building event, our team of twelve sat in a circle, and each of us had to say something positive and politely mention a weakness of every other individual in the room. Not easy to do or hear. But listen, we all did. There were plenty of tears. However, the vulnerability displayed by all team members went a long way to building trust. We developed a genuinely respectful and effective work environment because of her leadership. By all accounts, she set an excellent example.

In addition, two men in my life stand out as joyful leaders. Both left successful careers to set up charitable organisations that provide material and spiritual help to the less advantaged. These men and their spouses abandoned the comfort of a first-world society and immersed themselves in impoverished and war-torn third-world countries to help others. Their selfless acts and joyful countenance immensely impact me to this day. These two families sacrificed for others in such a way that they sought no personal favour or gain, yet they realised positive impacts in several highly disadvantaged communities.

I am truly honored to call these two men my friends. I often reflect on their behaviours and unselfish acts as examples of being joyful leaders. The outcome of their noble and cheerful lives continues to expand and impact hundreds, if not thousands. Theirs is the hallmark of good leadership. One of the outcomes of going through the ordeal with my sociopathic brother is that no matter what business challenge I faced after that numbing experience, nothing could ever faze me again. I had been through the worst and came out victorious on the other side. This mindset benefits me when chaos ensues all around. The source of my underlying joy is my newfound strength.

Another insight I came across was from a book by well-known author and commentator Andy Stanley entitled "The Best Question Ever". It focused on what questions you should ask yourself when faced with a daunting decision. His answer is deeply profound. "Based on your past experiences, current circumstances, and future hopes and dreams, what is the wisest thing to do?"[5] How does one know the wisest thing to do? Wisdom is accumulating experience and knowledge and intelligently applying this to any situation.

I have tried to remember this compelling question at home or work. It forces me to pause and think things through carefully. Compiling all my accumulated good and bad experiences and where I see my future going, "What is the wisest thing to do?" is a question I test myself with repeatedly.

I often thought about the wisest course of action to take in dealing with my father. Even though my parents' relationship was dysfunctional, I always felt that if anyone in our family dynamic should offer forgiveness to my Dad, it should come from my Mom.

For years, I felt this way; she was mistreated severely for the most part. After they divorced in year 37 of their marriage, I pulled away from my Dad, and consequently, so did my wife and children. Enough hurt had occurred, primarily from my father, and I didn't want any negative overflow of the divorce to impact my family.

Years went by without any interactions between my Dad and me. One day, I realised that I also had to forgive him, not for what he had done to my mother, but for what he did to my siblings and me by leading a life that was not the best example: indeed, quite an embarrassing one to me. Yet, I also concluded that I should ask him for forgiveness for breaking off our relationship over the years. I distinctly remember the moment I phoned him.

During a routine shopping trip, he and his new wife were in their vehicle waiting to cross the US-Canada border. When he answered, I asked for his forgiveness and forgave him. He cried! What an unexpected reaction! It was too much for me, and I sobbed too. He told me that I had nothing to be forgiven for, and he needed forgiveness. Although we can remember the past, we have forged a new path that has redeveloped and redefined our relationship.

The Bible tells us to honor our parents. It doesn't mean condoning whatever they may have done. It means for me or us to celebrate their lives by living a respectable life that brings them joy.

THE PAYOFF

Where does leadership begin? One would ask. If you have a family, your most important role is leading your family in a joyful environment. Family is the fertile training ground for all things related to leadership.

As I mentioned earlier, it still saddens me that I did not have a good role model growing up. As such, I aim to lead my family, hoping my children will respect and be proud of me.

Recalling Martin Luther King Junior's quote about excellence, he stated:

"If a man is called to be a street sweeper, he should sweep streets even as Michelangelo painted, or Beethoven composed music, or Shakespeare wrote poetry.

He should sweep streets so well that all the hosts of heaven and earth will pause to say, 'Here lived a great street sweeper who did his job well".[6]

My goal is to be something other than an executive manager, high-ranking business leader, or street sweeper! My focus is entirely on being the best family keeper, and my work is important but secondary. I want to be the best husband and father ever. While serving as an Air Force Captain, I was asked to attend Staff School. Attendance at this school was a necessary step to becoming promoted to Major. However, we had a baby and a toddler now, and going to Staff School would mean being away from my family for thirteen weeks. I said, "No, thank you." I knew my priorities and stuck by them. This philosophy paid dividends.

You have noticed that I hold up leadership with one's family as the key to establishing joyful leadership. Undoubtedly, we all lead different lives, and not all have families. However, the principles and actions discussed are transferable to all one's close relationships. One need not have a partner or children to establish a positive relationship in one's homely environment or community.

I remember being awestruck when I remembered a question I often posed to my young son. It's what any parent would ask. "What do you want to be when you grow up?" He always answered, "To get married and have a family." This response came from a soon-to-be young man who didn't focus on a position or career when asked but always defaulted to marriage and family.

His response validated my purpose of raising joyful children and setting an example of deep-seated contentment. That is what a leader must bring from their personal space to the workplace: an aura of deep-seated contentedness that cannot be displaced no matter the circumstances.

This mindset reminds me of a poem written by Edgar Guest entitled, "Am I True to Myself?"

"I have to live with myself, and so
I want to be fit for myself to know,
I want to be able, as days go by,
Always look myself straight in the eye;
I don't want to stand, with the setting sun,
And hate myself for the things I have done.
I don't want to keep on a closet shelf
Many secrets about myself,
And fool myself, as I come and go,
Into thinking that nobody else will know
The kind of man I am;
I don't want to dress up myself in sham.
I want to go out with my head erect,
I want to deserve all men's respect;
But here, in the struggle for fame and wealth
I want to be able to like myself.
I don't want to look at myself and know
That I'm bluster and bluff and empty show.
I can never hide myself from me;
I see what others may never see;
I know what others may never know,
I never can fool myself, and so,
Whatever happens, I want to be
Self-respecting and conscience free."[17]

I have broken the chains of my past. Even now, my son would say, "Dad, if I could only be half the man you are, I would be happy." Can you possibly imagine how that makes me feel? And by the way, my son is a wonderful husband and father to three handsome boys and is twice the man I am. We are each other's best friends. My beautiful daughter is a dedicated wife and mother of two gorgeous girls (with one more child on the way). They all live within minutes of us. My wife and I have recently retired and can now wholeheartedly enjoy the fruits of our joyful labour, teamwork, and leadership.

I may not be a leadership guru, but I have learned to look myself in the eye, not to doubt my self-respect, and to be secure in knowing that I know the true meaning of Joy and that others see it in me. That is my leadership secret.

CHAPTER SEVEN

"Being challenged in life is inevitable, being defeated is optional." – Roger Crawford.

CONQUERING YOUR OBSTACLES

by Martin Imlach

It's 3.15a.m. on a January morning with the wind blowing and the rain pelting against the window. I start looking back and trying to work out why I cannot sleep as usual. The last few years have been tough, but it was my torment and the highs and lows from my perspective of my little life experience.

I was the guy at school who wasn't "gifted" with wanting to learn academically. I was more of a hands-on guy who loved being and doing things like driving tractors and cars. Fortunately, I grew up around Engineers and weekend mechanics with a passion for traction engines, old tractors, and vehicles.

In the summer, I would be at a traction engine rally with my Dad and his mates until now, when I look back at how fortunate I was to be. You only really appreciate the upbringing you have once you are older.

With a background in engineering and my hands-on approach to life, I left school after a week of work experience at a Commercial vehicle dealership as a mechanic. I left school at age 15 on the 30 May 1991 and started in the dealership on the 2 June 1991, where I served my time for the next four years, which I thoroughly enjoyed and made lifelong friendships.

I met my first mentor, the workshop supervisor, who at the time was a neighbour and who lived across the street. He was steadfast and someone I have respected all my life. He told me often, **"You don't give up, and when the tough get going, you dig in and beat it."**

During my six years at the dealership as an apprentice, I did what I had to do: listen, learn, and speak when the time was right, and I learned life skills that would become the fundamental tools in my career. It was the break I wanted, my rite of passage, unlike these days where the same 'rite of passage' now is not extended to the youths of today.

Where I am from in the Northeast of Scotland, all the young folks and trades were going to work in the Oil and Gas sector where the big bucks were, and the saying about the town was, "Are you big in oil." So, as a "young loon" trying to impress the ladies, you had to be big in oil to meet women.

As it happened, this was the start of my journey of 24 years in a sector of the industry that would take me around the world and allow me to experience things many people would never have done, and I am humbled. If not for this career choice, I would have never met my wife.

I took a position as a mechanic within a service company providing cementing equipment and pumping equipment of cement, chemicals, and liquid Nitrogen to Oil majors. This was the start of the journey of discovery in this sector, full of characters and possibilities for making lifelong friendships.

I was taken into the office and handed my first-ever Notice letter, at which point I thought I'd failed to impress the management. Another two lads were given the same letter. So, what do I do? I thought about it for a while and spoke with the guys in the workshop and my mate, a former employee from another company that supplied lifting gear inspection services. He said, "We are looking for guys to work with us; this is my boss's number; call him in an hour after I talk to him about you and see what happens."

Hours later, I received a call from his boss asking me to go into their office after work. We briefly chatted, and thirty minutes later, I was employed to repair and inspect lifting equipment, which I was delighted to do at the time. I started my new job, stuck my head down, and worked away. Presumably, I must have done something right because after three months, I was asked to help the offshore inspection teams as they were short of guys, and I had my survival certification from my previous employment.

I went to a rig called the Murchison (aptly named the Hanoi Hilton for some reason); there were two of us, and I did what I had to do. I was hooked, and I enjoyed the work and the responsibility, and I now know the respect given to me by the crew. Things went well, and again, I was asked to go to another oil rig with another team. I was in, and off I went.I got a van that would take me around the city doing jobs in every industry sector, for the local government, and doing the rigging for theatres; it was great, and life was good. *But as the old saying goes,* **"All good things come to an end."**

For about a year, I worked day and night away for weeks. I worked something like 350 days, and I was dog-tired all the time as I was going from the US to home for a couple of days and then to the Far East and back to the States working 12–16 hours a day, then back to the rigs in the North Sea or any sea.

The airline loyalty cards were racking points; as we all know, points make prizes. But sadly, I was never at home and had to decide to end my relationship with another girlfriend. I returned to my old trade and secured a job working for a company that specialised in engines for industries from road transport to maritime and mobile electrical generators. It was varied work and, more importantly, a regular job where I had a life. Life was good.

Things appeared to have settled for a while, and then the dreaded letter came, and surprisingly, I was laid off again for the second time. I thought to myself, what am I doing wrong? It was time for self-introspection.

I saw an advert for a contract mechanic, so I applied and took an interview a week later. I was working again, this time at the main competitor of my first oil and gas job, doing the same type of work as everyone else. The routine of working in the workshop and offshore carrying out maintenance and repairs was good. It felt wonderful to be back doing what I loved; from there on, I was approached to join the project team installing and removing these systems and equipment. Without hesitation, I accepted the opportunity since I would have the chance to travel and work around the world again, which I was missing.

Interestingly, this was my first time working on projects. I loved the work; it was hard and at the same time rewarding, but it was a great feeling to complete a project and to have the self-satisfaction of saying to yourself, "I've done that!". It is where I found my place. Back then, the film "Titanic" was just released, and I watched it in the cinema with my girlfriend. If memory serves me well, it was around Boxing Day.

I recalled there was a part in the film, and a light bulb moment came to me. It was part of the film where the little submarine goes into the vessel's hull, called an ROV. I want to do that for a living, and if I see something I like, I go for it. "You don't give up." "When the tough gets going, you beat it."

One day, I was working on a rig installation from hell when things started to go wrong. I was thinking, "Why me." I had a chat with the equipment operator of the rig, claiming I had seen these ROVs, and I fancied a go at them. Doug mentioned that his sister works for a company in the Human Resources department, so I submitted my CV, not thinking I would get a chance to work there. Well, I was wrong. I was at home when I got a call asking if I would be interested in the job and that I should come for a "chat." So, I decided to go along for this unofficial chat with the manager of the ROV tooling dept.

During our conversation, the manager asked if I would be interested in joining the company, considering I had the necessary skills obtained throughout my career as a mechanic. "I go for mechanics as they are "jack of all trades," says he.

As luck would have it, this was an exciting opening in a field of work. Even now, I still find it fascinating, and this aspect of my career has stuck with me from 1999 forward to the present day.

It was the moment I developed my leadership experience and used it as a catalyst to further my career in management. It came about working in a remote part of the world and dealing with guys who were "up-man crews" in the trade, as I was part of the dedicated crew that operated and maintained the systems.

I had gone down to the remote region of West Africa as the ROV tooling specialist who dealt with all the tooling and tools employed on these ROVs, as there was limited space for the crews.

Time swiftly went by. I was the tooling technician, flying the ROV and developing my newfound expertise. I became the third man to operate and fly the ROV as part of the team. I was a jack of all trades, scrouging parts and tools from the guys on the rig to carry out repairs to the system to be the base mechanic repairing vans, trucks, and generators on the beach for the staff house as there was reliable electrical supply.

Life at this point was good. I was working six months of the year, and in my time off, I was driving a lorry for a haulage company, earning extra cash and my excuse to stay out of the pub.

I had been working in West Africa for three years, and taking preventive medication was taking its toll. I was worn out all the time and started to feel unwell. My girlfriend (now wife) had noticed my skin had gone from dark brown tanned from being in the sun all the time to going yellow. I went to see the doctor, who did some blood tests.

The doctor suggested that the symptoms I was experiencing were brought on by drinking, poor eating habits when I was away, and partying too hard at home (NOTE: this was NOT the case). Then, as always, the curve ball of life struck. I transferred to another project in a new country. I had to start building professional relationships with the guys all over again from working in the West African countries and being placed on projects in the North Sea, which I loathed.

At this point, I was working very closely with guys from other companies, carrying out interventions on their companies' equipment. We got acquainted, and I would speak with their boss before I knew it. Another opportunity presented itself: — — — — to take me into a new field of work and a new challenge that would lead me to work for myself as a consultant. Life was good; the money was good, and I was working my way up the management ladder from being a supervisor to acting as the client representative for the subsea aspect of the project. Once more, everything is going well.

I worked hard to get to this point in my career, but my education level needed to be improved. I was getting passed over for promotions, but I had found my sweet spot and was happy, or so I thought. At some point, the tiredness returned with a vengeance, and I was laid in bed with no energy and barely reached the toilet. I requested an in-house doctor visit, and the story 'You're Drinking Too Much' appeared again, where I pointed out I hadn't had a drink in four months because I was constantly feeling drained.

Three days later, the doctor referred me to the hospital for further investigation, which revealed that I had a condition affecting my blood called Hemochromatosis and that my liver had also been affected. Having Hemochromatosis means the body cannot process the iron in my diet, thus resulting in excess iron building up in my joints, causing extreme discomfort; this would explain why I was so tired, sleeping 18 hours a day at times. This lifelong condition can be treated by taking blood to remove the iron and diet changes, and the requirement to stop drinking (well, I still take a drink now and then).

With the condition under control again, I returned to work and took a role as Testing Manager, testing equipment before installation. I took to the role like a duck to water. I loved the position. It was my first job managing a team of guys, and I held full responsibility for the testing budget and management of the sites. To this point, I was the testing manager of a multi million-pound project, responsible for the whole project and managing multiple contractors and personnel at the height. I was looking after 120 guys on-site daily, accountable for all aspects and, most notably, their safety.

My past experiences had stood me in good stead as I could get the best out of the teams and deliver the projects on time and under budget. Then came the big nosedive in the fortunes of the oil and gas sector, and again, I was paid off like thousands of other people. I took some time out, regrouped my thoughts, and found a new role within the industrial sector. I took a role within the civil sector; there was the largest road project in Europe at the time, where I lived, and they were looking for personnel to do jobs for them. Fortunately, I met a recruiter who had faith in my skillsets. She placed me in a contract role doing some Quality Management and equipment compatibility reports for concrete production. I submitted my findings to the construction JV board and was asked to perform the required repairs and recommission the plants. At this point, I had to attend a meeting with the project director.

I was assigned a structural concrete production project manager position, and based on our conversation, the plants had been working at 20% capacity. I would also look after the concrete's transport and distribution as it operated at

15% of its capacity. I like the challenge! We set up a JV with a national concrete supplier in the first six months, opened a new transport and distribution system, and integrated a new team member. We set about daily changing things on the bounce, firefighting issues, and challenges.

My new partner had taken the plants from 20% capacity to running them at 90% capacity, integrating and expanding the team as we went along. It was an extremely stressful role that took its toll as we worked seven days a week, 16-18 hours a day. After nineteen months, I thought I had a heart attack, but thankfully, following my diagnosis in the hospital, I was suffering from a great deal of stress. It shook me to the core and my partner and best friend, a friendship forged in adversity.

If it were not for meeting Bruce, it wouldn't have happened; this is where I learned a few hard truths: We are human, we make mistakes, and you can only do what you can with what you have. Bruce and I worked long hours coordinating loads to the structure, operating the batching plants, and driving the trucks delivering the concrete.

Looking back, I feel a sense of gratitude for the achievements and friends I made along the way, even though it came to the detriment of my health. At this stage, I took the plunge and looked into further education to acquire the skills the job market demanded. I bounced about in driving jobs to keep myself busy and employed. Soon afterwards, I learned I had a brain tumour. I started to experience a sore head, became forgetful, and gained weight while the effects of having Hemochromatosis had set in.

I had regular check-ups because of this condition's side effects, meaning I have an 85% higher chance of getting liver cancer (thank God for the NHS). While on this subject, I asked the liver specialist nurses about this, and they suggested that further blood tests and an MRI would be required.

I attended numerous appointments and doctor visits only to be told I had a

Brain tumour in my Pituitary Gland, located in the centre of the brain at the top of the spinal cord and controls the weight and hormones of the body. The treatment I was to receive was a drug with side effects, which meant I would eventually have to stop taking it.

So, I was to have the tumour removed by surgery, and now that is a conversation, I never thought I would have. Three months later, I was due for surgery, a "keyhole" style operation that allowed the specialist to perform a procedure by going through the nose. Indeed, there were a few complications afterwards, but three months passed, and I recovered and returned to driving again.

I was back to being my old self. I enrolled in a Master's programme in Engineering Management at Hull University online, allowing me to work and study simultaneously. Still, as you have seen, I didn't make life easy at work.

I had an interview with Dr. Angeliki Papasava, and I knew from this meeting that this lady would profoundly affect my life. While studying, I secured a new role as a System Engineer within another oil and gas service company. Well, "That's another fine mess I got myself into again."

I knuckled down and worked to develop the required documentation and organise all the logistical requirements for testing and site set-up, as this would require testing sites in four locations. Then, to top it all off, the Covid-19 pandemic hit, and we all know how that affected everyone in the business and how we could operate, so it was another, shall we say, challenge that I had to overcome.

As the weeks progressed, I realised I was pretty good at formal education, attaining 85% in my first and 76% in the second modules. At last, I was completing my final module and preparing for my dissertation project when my mother became unwell and needed to be cared for in a residential care home, which undoubtedly added more pressure on the family.

Sadly, I lost my Mum on 23 December 2022, but before her passing, I made sure she knew I had completed my Master's study and graduated, from which I will take solace. She was proud of me for leaving school at fifteen and returning 32 years later to complete my formal education. The moral of a story is the lesson that the story teaches about how to behave in the world. Moral comes from the Latin word mores, for habits.

The moral of this story is that life circumstances may get in the way, but when the chips are down, it is all about how you choose to deal with them. The big question is, do you allow your adversities to make or break you as a person? I did everything well to get to where I want to be through hard work, a bit of luck, and the power of positivity and sheer doggedness! You learn from your mistakes. If you get put down, get back up and follow your heart; learn and embrace change, and don't be scared to take risks; make a change as you never know it could lead you to better and greater things and new experiences.

As I concluded, I pray that my story and experiences will help others navigate life and make a difference to someone or anyone in the smallest of ways. The thought of happiness for me, the guy who left school with not a lot to achieve the positions I have attained today and experience the things I have experienced.

I can only thank all who have helped and challenged me to change and use the power of collaboration to achieve incredible feats of personal pride and assist others. I am proud to be working with a charity set up by Dr. Mervyn to help people with brain tumours and their families, and I am pleased to be part of this new journey.

CHAPTER EIGHT

"Trust yourself. Create the kind of self that you will be happy to live with all your life. Make the most of yourself by fanning the tiny, inner sparks of possibility into flames of achievement". – Foster C. McClellan

BECOMING AN EMOTIONALLY INTELLIGENT LEADER

by Carey-Ann Thurlow

A good friend once told me that a "Master's Degree is never achieved independently." It takes an army of supporters, friends, family, colleagues, and a mindful determination to complete. He suggested that I purchase the frame for my Master's degree when I begin the program and write the name of every person who supported me, assisted me, and collaborated with me for the duration of the two and half years while completing my schooling. I still have that frame today, proudly boasting my MBA degree on the wall of the College I now own and operate.

The frame contains the names of my husband, my children, my close and extended family members, and friends who supported my every move. It includes the names of strangers I met at the University taking the same programme and acquaintances willing to lend their knowledge in specific areas of my studies.

I recall my second module at Roehampton University. I had just completed the first module on Leadership and achieved a first-class honours grade. Dr. Mervyn, one of our many professors, led our group with poise and passion. He had an excellent way of engaging our group and encouraging us to communicate and collaborate on our reading material.

We challenged one another's opinions, ideas, and hypotheses. We shared our thoughts and became better learners in the twelve weeks. It set me up for success, and I felt honoured to be a part of this beautiful community. Later in the MBA programme, I realised it spoiled me slightly, moving forward!

Then, we hit module two: Finance. It took me so far out of my comfort zone that I resorted to hiring tutors to get me through each section. One afternoon, a good friend took me downtown in Calgary near work to meet up with her husband, who had a keen eye for spreadsheets and numbers. After a three-hour session, I gained an understanding of the concepts I needed to learn to move through the online content myself. I consulted with fellow students, who had followed suit in hiring tutors to complete the module, and together, we made it through. There were many pots of coffee made to make it through the long days, module by module, paper by paper, and I headed for the finish line to complete my Master's degree.

Often, I was asked why I chose to take my MBA degree. While I found this an odd question, my only response was that I always wanted to achieve this goal, so I embarked on the journey of university education. I knew deep down inside that there was another reason, but I could only muster to say to people that I was crushing another goal on my bucket list.

With two children and a full-time job, my studies had to fit into my schedule. This chapter is about having the ability to work toward a goal, overcoming the odds, and building your future dream. Leadership came quickly to me from a young age. I was an athletic child and competitive child. I had no interest in coming in last in anything I did. I was a 'natural born leader.'

I completed high school at seventeen and entered post-secondary college as a Visual Communications - Display Major. It fed my artistic flair and became my first shot at becoming a higher educated version of myself. As I moved through college for Visual Communications and eventually into my first big job, it became clear that I wanted to make decisions and create a path for others. I worked my way up into management at a young age before deciding to embark on a career change to the dental industry.

Eager to start my life somewhere new, I moved to a small resort town called Banff in Alberta, a four-hour drive from home. I craved independence and focused on freelance work to earn more income at a young age. With visual display design in my back pocket, I did 'side hustles' for business storefronts around town. My entrepreneurial side had started to sprout!

For the next five years, I continued to work full-time while engaging in freelance work before moving into the dental industry. It was a complete change and quite a culture shock from the artistic version of myself. I had also moved up into management in my full-time career in retail, so leaving to embark on a new journey was a tad stressful! I had also started a family and had more than just myself to consider. Knowing this career move felt right, I quickly grew a desire to go back to school to further my way into dental assisting. Adversity was about to shine in full force.

As a single parent to my young son, I had to make intelligent choices for two. I continued working full-time in the dental industry while raising my child and returning to school via distance delivery to gain my education. It was long and wasn't easy, but it was worth it.

I recall many evenings of sitting down at the table to study at nine o'clock once I had put my young son to bed. I had worked all day, spent time with my son, and managed to get on a bike ride or two before settling into my studies. It was my only time to focus on the learning material and dive into the world of becoming a dental assistant.

On many evenings, I would study until eleven o'clock and then surrender myself to bed before repeating the same routine the next day. This became my life for the next two years. *Looking back today, I often wonder if I was living in survival mode. It was all I knew, and my vision remained strong to create an opportunity for a better life for my son and me.*

I completed the dental assisting program and eventually moved to the big city, where opportunity was abundant. I was beginning to realise my potential.

SUCCEED THROUGH PERSEVERANCE

After years of experience in the dental industry, I landed my dream job at a College in Calgary, where I first instructed in the dental assisting program. I eventually became the Chair of the Dental Health Department. I felt like I was finally there. Like I had just conquered it all: my goals, my dreams. This new reality of having it all set in nicely. I had an opportunity to combine my experience with my dental assisting and management education to inspire and mentor other students in the program.

I became involved in boards within the College and ventured into the world of regulatory boards and councils in the dental assisting industry. I volunteered and soaked up information and knowledge from anyone and everyone around me who was willing to share it with me. I recalled being asked 'why' I did so much at the time, yet it was a craving and a desire that did not feel like work. Being involved in my industry on a higher level fed my soul and improved my knowledge. I could not stop.

It wasn't long before I realised that my brain needed more, and my passion for returning to higher education was near. One afternoon, I passed a lovely booth set up in the hallways of my workplace, filled with pamphlets and information on various Universities. I stopped briefly to engage in discussion with the lady at the booth, only to find myself with 'imposter syndrome' and the thought that a degree just wasn't achievable for me. Little did I know then that this would be my path forward for the next few years. I researched universities in Canada, the USA, and overseas to find the best fit for me, and eventually enrolled in the MBA programme through the University of Roehampton in England.

With two children now and a full-time career, I knew I had to be strategic in how this played out in my everyday life; it was to be my second time taking a distance delivery program, but the stakes were very high this time. It meant sacrifice and determination. It meant some things had to give, including outings with friends and family. I was ready.

I was scheduled and consistent and always stayed on the end goal. I read articles at the football fields when my sons were doing their sports, and I wrote papers in my vehicle at any given time. I made pots of coffee after dinner on many evenings and settled down at the kitchen table with my laptop as I completed projects and lived on minimal sleep.

It was hard: - It was challenging - It was exhilarating. Nothing of this magnitude would come easy. I was committed to achieving greatness. And I wouldn't trade it for anything. I spent two and half years completing my MBA programme, including my thesis. I crushed it. I loved it. I had highs and lows, as all students do, and I was relieved when I completed the programme, but with mixed emotions.

My university study-buddy group had become my online family, and we were each other's network. From a distance, we held one another together and pushed for success.

While finishing one big dream, I was letting go of a community I cherished so dearly. Little did I know that these University friends would become lifelong confidants. Only one thing needed to be added: a new career path to help me achieve my next big dream and utilise all the knowledge I gained at university. I didn't quite know what that was yet. I knew I wanted to do something with education and stay in the dental industry. So, out I went to do some soul searching.

THE BIRTH OF RISIO

"Do the one thing you think you cannot do. Fail at it. Try again. Do better the second time. The only people who never tumble are those who never mount the high wire. This is your moment. Own it"
 - Oprah Winfrey

It was 29 August 2018. Casey and I met for dinner in a quaint little diner in downtown Calgary. Casey and I had known each other from our 'Banff days' and worked in a great little dental office there for nearly five years. We followed each other's paths through travel, education, family, and friendship. As we talked about where we were professionally and personally, we made our way to a conversation that would change our lives forever. That evening, at a table for two, we decided to open our Dental Assisting College.

It was mind-blowing! What started as a simple conversation about 'we should do this' became our most prominent dream. It suddenly became clear one evening how my years of volunteering, working full-time, and gaining higher education were finally about to pay off.There was never a question of 'what if'; instead, there was only a question of 'when.' Failing was never a part of our vocabulary.

Over the next two years, we worked endlessly to build the curriculum for an online learning dental assisting program that would span Canada. With my wide range of volunteering on various provincial and national boards, I gained the knowledge to navigate the program approval process with our regulators effortlessly. Casey and I spent months building the program's foundation, the online learning modules, evaluations, examinations, program and clinical policy manuals, and everything else that became a part of the program. *It was bigger and even more significant than we could have ever imagined.*

Casey and I were parenting, working other jobs (I had left the previous College I worked at to go back into the dental industry to manage Orthodontic practices in the city), and building our new school virtually. We had approval processes to follow, learning outcomes to consider, domain descriptions to cross-reference, and guidelines to meet. We were forced to revise and rebuild as we built the foundation and turned in material for approval. We were forced to add and delete learning content and challenge ourselves to think outside the box. We were challenged to stay true to our mandate and our vision, which was to offer access to education to those who could not leave their hometowns to attend a traditional dental assisting program.

We often went back to the drawing board to revisit our vision. And on many occasions, we wanted to quit. But that was never an option. Our hearts were invested, and through this program, we knew we would change the face of dental assisting education forever.

Our final approvals from our dental assisting regulator in Alberta, the National Board, and Alberta Advanced Education were in place in November 2019. For nearly a year and a half, while working alternate jobs and raising our families, Casey and I built this program and persevered through many long days and nights to complete it. We were ready to open our college and start living our dream. We were equipped and ready to prove we could do this.

The first intake of students began in January 2020, followed by the second intake in April 2020, followed by a worldwide pandemic. It hit the world like a ton of bricks, and every nation came to a standstill. Venues closed. Universities and Colleges closed, Restaurants and Malls. It appeared that everything was closing except our new dental assisting school.

We had already built our program to be online, so when the pandemic hit, and most universities had to transition their curriculum online, we were already ahead of the curve. Our school became very popular very fast. We had built a program for individuals in rural communities who wanted to maintain employment in a dental office while gaining their education online.

But as the pandemic lingered, weeks became months; our college soon became popular with those in the larger cities and further afield. We had registrations from all over Alberta, including neighbouring provinces. Our success skyrocketed, and we celebrated! Risio Institute for Digital Dental Education was booming!

FORGING AHEAD

In late 2020, I walked through our college doors, holding my dream on my shoulders while celebrating the success of our determination and hard work. My good friend and business partner, Casey Sharp, and I started with a vision two years earlier that was now our living reality.

We had secured a site in the south side of Calgary to host our on-site clinical training, which was expansive and modern. Over the next few months, we geared up for our first clinical module with our students while we cleaned, renovated, and prepared for another milestone. We had no idea that day that this was about to get big, fast. We had yet to determine that the current economic conditions would skyrocket our full business forge ahead. We had just learned how much support our dental community would provide us when the phone calls, emails, website visits, and social media ratings flooded in. Now, the real work was about to begin. Casey and I worked full-time for Risio Institute and offered our students the best possible experience from registration to graduation.

Our vision for Risio Institute for Digital Dental Education was to provide access to education for everyone. We wanted to provide access to dental employees in small towns who could not move to the city to get their education. We wanted to provide access to education to single moms, parents, and newcomers to Canada and provide the highest quality of service in the Dental industry, much better than the services available.

Our online format provides all of this and more. Furthermore, it allowed students to maintain employment while gaining their education. It provided an opportunity for dentists to retain their great employees. It was a 'win-win' for us all.

With the popularity of Risio Institute rising, Casey and I knew we needed a game plan and a five-year goal chart. Our next dream was to focus on the five-year plan and build additional programs under the Risio umbrella, which meant hiring employees with our vision to carry on the daily tasks within the dental assisting program. In so doing, it would allow us to put our creative skills to work again and continue to build. In August 2023, we launched our second Risio location in Canada: Toronto! And so, the growth phase begins!

LEAD WITH PASSION

Becoming a leader may come easy to some, but becoming an emotionally intelligent leader is on another level. Building our school came with its own set of hurdles. Previous employers fought for copywriting to curriculum development. We consistently proved our new ideas, worth, and value.

We overcame the obstacle of having a third partner in our company early on, whom we eventually bought out due to irreconcilable differences. We had to overcome these circumstances and challenges to lead us to the larger picture. We had to rise above and be emotionally intelligent about our dealings with others who brought forth these challenges. Only some things were easy. The time spent away from my family and friends is irreplaceable. Volunteering on provincial and national boards meant time away from my children. While I gained knowledge in various aspects of my career, I lost irreplaceable time with my loved ones.

Perseverance is a word that I do not take lightly. It is the foundation of my very being. Frankly, nothing of great value comes easy, but your vision can become your reality with patience and determination.

Sometimes we don't quite see it. Occasionally, our path forward isn't in our line of vision; instead, it is in our subconscious minds. Even if you can't quite put your finger on it, it all begins with an idea and a dream. Persistence is crucial: rising to the challenge and finding ways to alter your lifestyle to fit it all in. Today, you can still find me on the football field with my laptop, but with different work.

While writing this chapter, I am completing the Dissertation for my Ph.D. in Higher Education: Governance, Policy, and Leadership! And it all started with a dream! We do the things we love to get to the places we need to be. We need passion to succeed. Lead from the heart. Everything else will follow. Believe in yourself, become A DOER, get out of your comfort zone, get out there, and DO it!

CHAPTER NINE

"I'm not afraid of dying. I'm afraid not to have lived." - Wim Hof

HELPING PEOPLE TO HELP THEMSELVES

by Dr Kieran Mervyn

My mother, Marie Teresa Mervyn, was born on 31 December 1947 and gave birth to me, the second oldest of six, on 31 December 1974. My Grandmother was Maltese. After marrying my grandfather, Malachy McCullough, they raised 13 children between three local communities – Ardoyne, Ballymurphy, and the Falls Road. My mother was the oldest.

Paddy, my father, was the youngest of 11 children. Locals often joked how 'there were no televisions in those days.' My father's close friend had 11 sons with red hair, and a lady from the Lower Falls had 21 kids, so full houses weren't unusual.

My father passed away in April 2023, so the timing of this chapter seems even more appropriate. He was a good man but enjoyed a life of excess. Puffing cigarettes from seven years old, he soon encountered Guinness and hardly lived a day without a pint of the black stuff until he transitioned to the spirit world.

One of his claims to fame was never having drunk a glass of water. I can't recall a time when he drank a glass of water, but he certainly had his share of uisce beatha, as we call it in Irish Gaelic (whiskey, 'water of life' which is derived from the Old Irish uisce (water) and beatha (life)). So, his passing wasn't a surprise by any stretch of the imagination but still laced with immense sadness. However, finding my 11-year-old daughter Cara's lifeless body a few years earlier, on 29 December 2019, was haunting.

The experience has nudged me from my comfort zone, making me more assertive and outspoken about brain disease and the lack of funding and support for brain tumour patients and families. I am now dedicated to raising awareness and funds to support our cause through the **Is Mise Cara Brain Disease Foundation**. Sharing this transformational story has helped me gain a much-needed sense of perspective and purpose.

Born into a conflict in the North of Ireland, I witnessed chaos and carnage from a young age. There always seemed to be something significant happening in the streets of West Belfast. My father's cousin was executed in his living room just a five-minute walk from our home in front of his young son, Sean. It was a random sectarian attack in broad daylight in the summer of 1989. Ironically, I'd just returned from a six-week cross-community trip to Virginia, USA. My father's first words at the airport were, 'Our Sandy's Dead.' Sean now seems to have overcome some of his adversities by becoming a leading defense barrister.

Another serious event occurred when my friend Ciarán (Kieran and Ciarán both sound the same; mine is the Welsh version of Ciarán) and I were seven and eight years old, respectively. We heard (what sounded) like an explosion, then cheering, and decided to investigate. Ciarán was like a whippet and outraced me every time, so he sprinted ahead.

Upon reaching Beechmount Avenue, I noticed the police and army firing baton rounds at protesters. After seeing the sparks fly amidst a whiff of sulphur, I deviated from the danger to play football on a different street. *Later that evening, I could hear someone shout, 'Kieran Mervyn's been shot.'*

After appearing on the scene, tenacious local women soon circled me, baffled by how I was still alive and breathing. Shortly afterward, we heard that Ciarán had sprinted onto the avenue before being shot and injured by the army. A local family from Amcomri Street hoisted him before calling for an ambulance. Some locals still mistake who was shot to this day.

Many similar events occurred throughout my teenage years, including multiple hostage-taking experiences at home, a family house fire and relocation, road accidents, and witnessing numerous violent incidents and deaths. So, I decided to follow my friend and his girlfriend to Florida for a job and a change of scenery.

After traveling to and from the United States (since the early 1990s), I realised in 1999 that another change was needed to develop myself. In California, many hours were spent discussing my life options with a good friend, Gary Kelly, who subsequently guided me through the application process for an Undergraduate Politics degree at Liverpool John Moores University. Liverpool was a great student city; nonetheless, navigating my way around the city as a Manchester United supporter felt tricky. I met my wife Faye in 2000, who'd just finished a Sociology degree at the same University. We went on to live in Leeds, where I completed my MSc in e-Commerce and PhD in Mobile Information Systems and Social Exclusion. My doctoral research into digital inequalities took me to locations including women's refuges (central offices), Muslim Forums, and Gujarat Hindu Societies, where I first-hand observed the realities of social and digital exclusion in underserved communities experiencing poverty and deprivation.

CARA'S PREMATURE BIRTH

After marrying Faye (July 2005 in Cuba) and experiencing the buzz of Havana, we were delighted to welcome our firstborn, Cara Mia, into the world on 12 February 2008. She'd arrived 11 weeks early, premature. Her original birth date was 30 April 2008, and her brother Finn was born on 30 April 2015. Weeks spent in neonatal were followed by several years in and out of the hospital with frequent bacterial and viral infections and significant surgical operations to address a narrow airway problem.

Faye worked at Leeds Met University throughout Cara's health challenges, and I was grass-hopping between small bits of teaching and research at Leeds and Bradford Universities. Later, I became a research and management consultant and Co-Director of Finncara Consulting Ltd (previous Co-Director of AM2 Partners Ltd).

One satisfying moment was completing a mixed-methods study on behalf of a local charity for their Big Lottery bid for a social exclusion project. The Government granted £9.8m to support people with multiple and complex needs through our intervention. My colleague Dr Nii Amoo (Nii) and I accepted the project on a shoestring budget because we had just registered AM2 Partners Ltd. We decided to use our knowledge and experience to help the charity struggling for funds.

After completing the research, Nii and I delivered the report to an audience of central government decision-makers at St Georges' Crypt in Leeds. It was great to hear that the charity received a grant of almost ten million pounds.

By a strange twist of fate, I was involved in an incident just yards from the scene of the presentation. One quiet Sunday morning, as Faye, Cara, Finn, and I crossed the bridge at the main hospital in Leeds, we noticed a commotion at the midpoint section where the dual carriageway passed beneath. A young lady was positioned on the far side of the bridge wall, ready to leap onto busy oncoming traffic. A wiry older man was leaning and gripping her but was clearly struggling. After spotting the danger, Faye took Finn's pushchair as I sprinted and lent my support. The lady cursed and screamed 'Let me Jump'; 'Leave me Alone' as I clasped her arm and shoulder.

A priest then appeared and quickly calmed her down. All three of us then hoisted her back over the wall to safety, and off they went to a church just meters away. Instinct took over that morning. It happened so quickly, but must have felt like an eternity for the lady. Cara was spooked by the event and often discussed her in conversations afterwards.

Cara's health problems continued to flare, and she frequently experienced bouts of sleep apnoea. There were often tired faces each morning. In a teaching capacity, more university students were accessing higher-level education through online channels, which enabled me to work from home, care for Cara, and spend precious time together. Cara still had a tracheotomy tube at the time of my PhD graduation.

After decannulation and a period of stability by Cara's standards, things seemed to fall into place (new house, new job) before something unforeseen emerged. She was diagnosed with a brainstem tumour at nine years old, just days before a planned three-week holiday to Majorca. The brainstem is situated where the brain connects with the spinal cord. We were devastated when Cara's neurologist explained the implications of the diagnosis and how the brainstem controls essential critical functions, including breathing and heartbeat. It felt like the end of the world for us both.

Tumours that develop in the brainstem are complex and challenging to treat. Even the gentlest of touches from a neurosurgeon to acquire a sample can be dangerous. This is necessary to check the type and level of aggressiveness. Any intervention in the stem area can cause death, blindness, or significant neurological damage. Cara almost died during the biopsy as they took the 6th sample.

After surgery, she'd had a premonition where she saw me and Faye stroll from the theatre after she'd witnessed her passing. Weeks later, she dreamed of seeing herself inside a pink coffin. For 15 minutes, we fought to resuscitate Cara before our four-year-old son, who stood on her bed and said, 'It's too late, Daddy; Cara's away to Heaven.'

We have experienced supernatural and paranormal activity around our home and beyond since Cara passed, which we have captured and shared in our two publications. Cara's priest, Father Emmanuel, was invited to our house after Cara's funeral and observed the ghostly activity. He subsequently participated in developing and promoting our first book, *Is Mise Cara: Orbs, Souls, and Holy Ghosts*. In appreciation, we printed 1,100 books in Nigeria, and the proceeds from sales will be donated to Father Emmanuel's charity and the broader community in Lagos and Abuja.

Lorna Byrne, a spiritual messenger and international bestselling author, is heavily involved in our publications. In the first book, Lorna explains how she met Cara on the other side. Others (mainly family) have experienced sightings of Cara, which may seem bizarre until you navigate through our book and Cara's story.

Upon completing our second book, *Signs from Cara and Beyond: Messages from the Spirit World,* the Charities Commission confirmed registration of the *Is Mise Cara Brain Disease Foundation.* We have completed Spanish, Chinese (Mandarin), and Irish language versions of our first book, and Spanish, Hindi, and Brazilian Portuguese versions of the second book are under construction.

Maria de Kannon Clè, the Director of Brains Get Famous in Madrid, is completing the Spanish version of Is Mise Cara, and audio book versions of our second book are forthcoming, too. Determined to leave a legacy for

Cara, we registered the Is Mise Cara Brain Disease Foundation in September 2022 www.carabraindiseasefoundation.com

During the tracheotomy years, Cara received a day or two monthly at a children's assisted living centre in Leeds. Anyone born in a different postcode area, e.g., Bradford, was often unable to access respite services. I'm grateful that my support provided to colleagues, students, and friends over the years is being returned through the implementation of our foundation.

We are fortunate to have a network of deeply committed individuals who are learning and growing themselves while enabling the Foundation to achieve its goals. In my capacity as CEO of the foundation, we will raise awareness of brain disease and use royalties from our publications for patient respite and family holidays.

HELPING OTHERS TO OVERCOME AND BECOME

As module leader on the Coaching, Mentoring, and Development module at the University of Law, London, I am often asked for practical tips and suggestions for dealing with work, life, and study pressures.

I encourage students wishing to grow and develop personally and professionally to follow Foggs' Tiny Habits programme. Before identifying three tiny habits to pursue, budding managers and leaders should self-reflect and read short articles on transformation.

One tip is to undertake self-analysis, e.g., around managerial role gap analyses, from which they should choose three or four areas to address. These often include decision-making skills, negotiation skills, or disturbance handling. I guide students in managing themselves by developing reflective, action-orientated, collaborative, and analytical mindsets. Once they identify their skills gaps, we can create an action plan for self-improvement.

Many thousands of scientific, peer-reviewed studies demonstrate the effectiveness of Mindfulness for coping with life challenges. Most international students who experience life in London, Manchester, and Birmingham for the first time greatly appreciate my coaching and mentoring.

They often mention works from one author, David Hawkin (RIP), that help them acclimatise to the master's programme and become more resilient. Hawkins' books, such as Power v Force and Letting Go, are summarised by the Indian coach Sunny Sharma, whose YouTube channel contains many great resources for anyone struggling with life. I turned to meditation after encountering sleepless nights during Cara's many years of disability, the brainstem tumour, and subsequent grief. Finding Cara that fateful night and battling to save her was horrific. We'll never forget it. Meditation was a Godsend and improved our sleeping habits and general well-being. Ten minutes of focused meditation before sleeping and first thing in the morning made me grateful to be alive and able to cope with the fast-paced world of teaching and research while grieving. Some breathing techniques were particularly helpful. Research shows that meditating lowers cortisol and, thus, overall stress levels.

My old mentor Terry Boyle (RIP) (who found his daughter Amy Lyn's body hanging) was sceptical. Still, he tried the 4-7-8 breathing technique with a blood pressure machine and became an avid follower, seeing dramatic health benefits.

Terry had a remarkable career but had never published in an academic journal. So, after working on a global healthcare project, I was proud to co-author a peer-reviewed article with Terry shortly before he died. Terry helped me and Faye through the loss of Cara, and his spiritual guidance was steadfast.

Since Cara's passing, I have followed "The Iceman" Wim Hof's cold method. Hoff is a leader in studying and practicing cold therapy for enhanced physical and mental health. Wim Hof's achievements include:

- *Running a half marathon above the Arctic Circle, barefoot, only wearing shorts*
- *Swimming underneath ice for 66 meters*
- *Hanging on one finger at an altitude of 2,000 meters*
- *Climbing the highest mountains in the world while wearing only shorts*
- *Running a full marathon in the Namib Desert without drinking*
- *Standing in a container while covered in ice cubes for extended periods.*

Scientific evidence shows that the autonomous nervous system, related to an innate immune response, can be wilfully influenced and is something previously unknown to science[1].

I have been teaching and supervising Postgraduate and Undergraduate students since 2008. Many appreciate my coaching and mentoring approach, and in 2023, I coached over 2,000 students in individual sessions. I learned a lot from the process too, so we grow together through personal and professional development. Most students are incredibly bright and well-educated in their home countries, so they are brilliant to work with. Over the years, I have taught an intricate mix of senior executives, traditional managers, and less fortunate students sponsored through NGO programmes and, in one case, an ex-child soldier. In a previous University coaching role, in 2015, during fascinating discussions that spanned themes such as poverty and deprivation, dealing with grief, illness, and depression, one student candidly explained how he was snatched from his home in Liberia and, within months, had subsequently... *"...executed so many people that he'd lost count".*

He was forced into war after his parents were kidnapped. Barely a teenager, he was rescued by an NGO and returned to his community, where he now plays a strategic role in local charity work. His peers looked bemused but simultaneously praised him for transforming himself. Most understood the context of his actions but struggled to place themselves in his shoes.

Another fascinating conversation occurred with a Malawi student who runs an orphanage with his wife. His dissertation topic was digital inequalities in Malawi and the prospect of introducing digital money platforms. The IMF states that Malawi is an agro-based economy. Fifty-seven percent of the rural citizenry live in poverty, and 25 percent live below the poverty line. So, the impact of poverty and financial exclusion is less in areas with high agricultural activity.

... Nkhotakota is the poorest district in the central region of Malawi[2] and Mulanje in the south. I am keen on conducting my research in the district as it will be closer to representability than in Nathenje, where, although there are poor people and households, they are not classified as the poorest. At more than 200 kilometres, Nkhotakota is very far from my home. I would have to make accommodation, meals, and transport provisions to go there. On the other hand, Mulanje is over 400 kilometres away and is notorious for killing strangers who are often suspected of bloodsucking [as confirmed by the U.S. Embassy in Malawi" [3]]. This is a practical challenge for me for the time being.

A message arrived shortly afterward about his near-death experience. After interrogation, he was accosted by an angry mob, believing that he had evil intentions. In this deeply religious community of Malawi, locals often refer to a biblical statement concerning new forms of money threatening their communities and how someone would appear like a "wolf in sheep's clothing."

Malawians often mistrust the concept of digital banking and prefer to hide their savings in personal spaces, which leads to frequent robberies and thefts. The student continued:

... Because we have been giving relief and poverty alleviation resources and running a school feeding programme in a distant village, they thought I had come to register beneficiaries for social cash transfer. It was chaotic – people pushing to be 'registered' and some snatching the questionnaires. Luckily, there were no

injuries, and no other personal property was stolen. I had informed the [village] chiefs earlier that I was coming to do academic research, but it seems the people did not believe them...

Through a bizarre chain of events, I taught several postgraduate students who lost loved ones in tragic accidents. One student was in a famous canoe race in South Africa when his double canoe flipped and trapped his girlfriend beneath. He survived and shared supernatural signs about his partner in our book *Signs from Cara and Beyond.* Other students recently lost loved ones and feel confident to share their experiences. So, it's remarkable how so many can find solace in grief with the proper support. I've included these students in several projects, including this book and journal publications.

As a senior academic, empirical evidence is essential for sense-making. However, sceptics and critics could enhance their curiosity and become more open to the spirit world. Famous psychiatrists such as Prof Ian Stevenson have scientifically explored the afterlife over many years. Stevenson undertook meticulous studies of children's memories of previous lives, e.g., via this example case below:

In Sri Lanka, a toddler once overheard her mother mentioning the name of an obscure town (Kataragama) that the girl had never been to. The girl informed the mother that she drowned there when her "dumb" (mentally challenged) brother pushed her into the river, that she had a bald father named "Herath" who sold flowers in a market near the Buddhist stupa, that she lived in a house that had a glass window in the roof (a skylight), dogs in the backyard that were tied up and fed meat, that the house was next door to a big Hindu temple, outside of which people smashed coconuts on the ground.

Stevenson confirmed that there was, indeed, a flower vendor in Kataragama who ran a stall near the Buddhist stupa whose two-year-old daughter had drowned in the river. At the same time, the girl played with her mentally challenged brother. The man lived in a house where the neighbours threw meat to dogs tied up in their backyard, and it was adjacent to the main temple where devotees practiced a religious ritual of smashing coconuts on the ground.

The little girl did get a few items wrong, however. For instance, the dead girl's Dad wasn't bald (but her grandfather and uncle were), and his name wasn't "Herath"—that was the name of the dead girl's cousin. Otherwise, 27 of her 30 idiosyncratic, verifiable statements panned out. The two families never met, nor did they have any friends, coworkers, or other acquaintances in common, so if you take it all at face value, the details couldn't have been acquired in any obvious way.

My daughter Cara's surgeon was once praised by his anaesthetist as '*the only person I know who knows their mind.*' As Lorna Byrne often explains, we are sparks of light from God, separate from mind and body. Upon death, our souls return home. Away from this physical world yet, paradoxically, never really leaving us, as we have noticed in recent years since Cara *transitioned* to the spirit world.

My wife and I believe everyone receives signs after losing a loved one. But most seem oblivious or dismissive of supernatural phenomena, which is unfortunate. In our first book, we sought alternative perspectives from people of different faiths and none to widen the conversation about life and the afterlife.

After so many responses from people who read Is Mise Cara, we compiled the second book based on their testimonies. Being vocal about grief and the supernatural and paranormal activity that ensued wasn't easy, because of the nature of the topic.

So, thank you for reading my story, which shares a blend of my academic and personal life experiences. In memory of Cara, our charitable foundation will help support, empower, restore, and socially include persons living with or affected by brain disease by providing opportunities for vital respite, relaxation, and family time. Perhaps my insights will help others overcome adversities and feel more peaceful in these turbulent times. Enabling people to learn and grow in a safe space is immensely rewarding.

Everyone should practice the art of reflection and foresight to foresee any future consequences of their actions [4]. We should continually develop ourselves and strive to inspire others where appropriate. Interpersonal and human relations are just as (if not more) important as technical skills for successful individuals, teams, and organizations.

So, too, is the ability to self-reflect. Over time, I have learned not to "correct" people, but rather to help them to see the error of their ways, just as Brockbank says, "the role of managers is not to achieve perfection, certainty or singular clear direction. Rather their role is to cope and enable others cope". I've tried to demonstrate my strengths, weaknesses, and commitment to continuous self-improvement in this story. Margolis [5] advises:

Shift[ing] from reflexive thinking to active thinking about how best to respond, asking themselves what aspects they can control, what impact they can have, and how the breadth and duration of the crisis may be contained.

The point of my story is to show that it's possible to grow from adversity and help others in the process. Terry J Boyle's (RIP) learning ensued until his last days on earth. He continued to share wisdom and advice, even as his health deteriorated. Terry and I both found the lifeless bodies of our daughters in Leeds and Ontario respectively, but we were determined not to let the experiences hold us back.

I now leave you with words from my brother. Damien reflects on his travels around the island of Ireland with his eight-year-old son Emmet.

"Me and my Dayo ... I try to do everything with him, sharing what I know and see. Colours of the rainbow of life and the different perspectives. People, nations,

Muslims, Hindus, Buddhists, Jews, Christians, Folk religionists and of course the religiously unaffiliated. The periodic table is in reverse. Give respect and compliments far and wide. Two men are looking through bars; one sees mud, the other the stars. Gaze in awe..."

CHAPTER TEN

"It does not matter how slowly you go so long as you do not stop." – Confucius

OVERCOMING AND BECOMING

by Rohan Johnson

Trials and tribulations are no respecter of "person". Honestly, adversities do not care about who we are or much about age, status, wealth, or gender. Sometimes, the only thing that matters is how one fights back. In difficult situations, we often do not realise that our challenges are merely opportunities for transformation. When we must deal with Life's struggles, we never know if we are being moulded for more extensive and incredible things ahead.

Life may throw us more than we can handle, and suddenly, your high status and position become irrelevant. Like a towering tree falling over time, the strongest of us may eventually fall. But unlike that "towering" tree, we are innately gifted with the ability to get back up, stand firm, and press forward no matter how challenging our circumstances. Indeed, some of our best opportunities are often packaged and wrapped up in challenging circumstances, hardship, and pain, if you can see.

As a child, whenever I saw an airplane flying above, I would tell myself that one day, I would fly away in that thing and go to "Foreign." For my siblings and me, "Foreign" was another place across the ocean where airplanes go. On 19 July 1998, at age 26, I left Jamaica destined for the United Kingdom with no more than £500 sterling in my wallet and a single suitcase.

Being young and ambitious, six months in the UK should be a long time to work hard and make enough cash to return to my home country and start my own business. But life had other plans for me. You see, although I was young and ambitious, I was not a risk-taker, which meant I would have to work within the confines of the law, but much more challenging to achieve my goal. It was not easy growing up in Jamaica and having been exposed to crimes, gun violence, and being shot at. I believed I was ready for anything London would throw at me. After all, London was not Kingston, so what could intimidate me? But, of course, what did I know about life within a foreign country? Very soon, life itself would become my greatest mentor.

Just six weeks after entering the United Kingdom, I was houseless and without work, and for the first time, I succumbed to living conditions that were inconceivable to me as a young man. Life was now taking me into uncharted territories. It was now 28 September 1998, just a little over nine weeks since entering the United Kingdom, and I was without shelter or a place to lay my head.

For a while, I thought, today is my 27th birthday, and no one knew where I was at that moment or what I was doing. I was fortunate to have found shelter, comfort, and a place to rest my head inside a public park restroom in North London. At last, I have a place to rest.

Newspapers kept me warm at night and magazines I used as a pillow. August and September were not usually cold, but I was still trying to acclimatise to their weather conditions. Having lived in Jamaica since birth, I was accustomed to a much warmer climate, but tonight, on my birthday, I felt cold as I lay there reminiscing on the past while residing in Jamaica. I thought about the beautiful moments during my tenure as a "Production Coordinator" and felt mortified about my unfortunate circumstances.

Throughout the night, I asked myself many questions repeatedly without having an answer, and then a "whisper" came to me; it said, "This is where you are meant to be." That night seemed to last forever, and I felt defeated. As a Jamaican, I was no stranger to life's harsh realities, but I needed to understand the harsh realities of life within a foreign country. But as you can imagine, I would be taught a lesson that would stand with me forever. I prayed for strength and courage to persevere. I knew that moment would pass, as nothing lasts forever. I had no intention of quitting.

The following morning, I woke up and smiled because it was a new day; the sun was shining and warm. I was humbled and rebounded two weeks after my sobering experience. Finally, I got a job and a place to sleep, and life improved. With each passing day, I grew stronger, knowing that this was one of life's experiences I would eventually overcome. I was determined not to allow this temporary event to defeat my purpose. I chose to overlook my struggles and regard my obstacles as necessary ills to reinforce my determination to achieve my goals.

As the months passed, things appeared to be going well, but then again, life always seems to have some good old hammer just waiting to knock YOU down. However, little did I know that all this time, I was going through a process of transformation that would prepare me for far more significant challenges to come. Sixteen months after overcoming my first trial, my grit and resilience to navigate life was about to be tested again.

By mid-February 2000, I was now considered an illegal alien in my new home and would be detained for five months afterward. Perhaps I could say that day one of my detention was hell itself. Suddenly, I lost my freedom. Eleven days into captivity, I was at my lowest point, but praying became my only option. I prayed until my detention center became my Palace. What relief I felt after two and a half hours of prayer. I was in captivity for the first time, yet I was free. But still, I questioned myself: why must I face these battles? And once more, I heard the "whisper" and knew I was at the right place and time. I was comforted. Right then, I knew there was a purpose for my life, and deep inside, I felt everything was happening just as intended.

Indeed, our trials can be overwhelming at best, and we often think they are too many for one person to conquer, but we can decide how life's situations will impact "self." I now understand that deep within, there lies greatness, and if used correctly, life can turn out exactly how you want it to be, irrespective of the highs and lows, given that, our strength to overcome life's obstacles rests in our ability to endure hardship and our capacity to prevail over adversities. Regardless, we can make better use of our adverse experiences, embrace them, and remain grateful.

That said, after five months, I was free again to roam the streets of London. In September of 2000, with the encouragement and support of a remarkable, loving, and caring Irish woman (who later became my spouse), it was time to embark on another journey to begin the next chapter.

I arrived on the Irish shores where Life's transformation truly began; indeed, the trials continued to show up, and I continued to prevail. I was determined to press on and keep moving, no matter the obstacles.

Having arrived in Cork, there was a sense of tranquility, and I noticed the landscape had striking similarities, which reminded me of my home country. Back then, the Irish were extraordinarily curious and friendly, particularly the Corkconians. By mid-2001, my former spouse gave birth to our only child, our son, Jake, when I was desperately trying to build a career and find employment to support my family.

Thinking back, I thank God I was present for the birth of our son. It was a beautiful yet surreal, life-changing experience to witness your child, another human being, brought into this world. At first, parenting was challenging, especially for my former spouse, a first-time mom, but as the old saying goes, "every dark cloud has a silver lining." We were blessed to be parents, and by a stroke of luck, I secured my first employment following the birth of our son. In an instant, my career took off with the help and guidance of some outstanding Corkconians. Every step of the way, someone was more than willing to assist.

By 2003, I was now an Irish citizen and dreamed of owning my first home, which would come through a year later. Regardless of past challenges and pitfalls, life was getting better. Ireland is truly the land of opportunity, and so far, Cork has been good to me and would reward me accordingly.

As the years passed, I had a family and a well-paid job working with an outstanding company. I am grateful to my former employer and employment because I probably wouldn't have seen more countries and cities worldwide than anticipated without this beautiful opportunity.

On reflection, migrating to Cork, Ireland was one of the most significant and life-changing decisions ever. I was blessed and proud to be Irish, and I wanted to extend that opportunity to a child I had considered my daughter since 1997. In early 2012, I travelled to Jamaica to pay respect to my deceased father and decided to begin the visa application process to give my daughter a shot at the Irish dream.

Swiftly, she was granted a Join Parent visa and would be arriving at Dublin Airport sometime in August 2012. By September, she was now a prominent secondary school student, where she excelled in her classes, and I was very proud of her achievements.

How quickly time flies: By 2015, she wanted to visit her mom during the summer holidays. Around 24 June 2015, while she was in Jamaica, she sent photos captured that day. I was happy at first, but those photos were strikingly eye-catching. For several minutes, I stared at those photos, and the more time I spent looking at them, the more I couldn't see any physical resemblance between myself and her.

I suddenly remembered that shortly after her birth, there were rumours that she may not be my biological daughter. Curiosity and anxiety rippled through my being as reality hit home that the child, I had raised for all those years might not be mine. My heart palpitates, and for moments, I contemplated telephoning one of my six sisters about my concern. Eventually, I mustered the courage and placed that dreaded phone call.

Without hesitation, after greeting my sister, I asked her if she believed I was the child's natural father, but to my surprise, my sister paused and asked me to give her a minute just for her to move to a better location for some privacy. I waited a few seconds, which felt like an eternity.

In her own words, she said, "Brother, I wondered how much longer it was going to take you to ask this question." Sparing no time to lose, my sister dropped that bombshell and confirmed my suspicion. I recalled asking her why anyone didn't mention this before. But in her low-pitched voice, "Brother, I wanted to tell you, but everyone, including Mom and Dad, said it wasn't my business to disclose such information." I thought, how could this be possible? I froze; I was numb and went stone cold for months.

For the remainder of 2015, my pride and ego tormented and handicapped me. I was a very proud man, and I refused to seek professional help or therapy or, even worse, share my situation with a stranger. I suppressed my grief and pain and tried to cope as best as possible, turning to alcohol, self-medicating, or consuming illicit substances. Naturally, I did whatever it took to numb up the pain. At the same time, I was enrolled at the University of Roehampton, London, but it was a challenge to continue studying while effectively serving my employer.

By early May 2016, my mentor (a brother from a different mother, as he would say) had died. I believe his death was due to excessive use of alcohol. As we were very close, I thought and felt somewhat responsible that I could not prevent his demise, or at least I blamed myself for not doing more for a dear friend. His newfound dangerous habit firmly held him and, in the end, got the better of him.

In all this turmoil, everything was becoming too much to handle. I was frustrated and feeling hurt; I wanted to surrender. I no longer wanted to "Be". The more I contemplated "surrendering" my life, the more I became comfortable with the idea. My heart just wasn't in it. Nothing mattered anymore; I did not care what my friends or family would think and how they would feel. I was just fixated on taking the easier way out.

Then, on 5 August 2016, it was a Friday, and at some time after 8p.m., I felt wonderfully calm inside because I had already decided that the time to check out was now. I had no fear whatsoever, and I did not give a toss about how anyone would feel after the fact. However, my effort to end it was futile; it was not my time, and I had not yet fulfilled my purpose in Life.

The following morning, I was hospitalised for approximately three weeks. While in the hospital, I met some wonderful and caring doctors, therapists, support staff, and others going through similar life struggles. When you think you have seen it all, life has a strange way of playing those gotcha games. It's like a rollercoaster: -today, you are up, and tomorrow you are down.

But honestly, life does not promise us a smooth journey. If nothing else, life has taught me that not all my days will be pain-free, or everything will go according to plan. It just does not go that way. It's imperative that one must learn how to ride through the storms of life and continually trust that there is a power "deep within" more significant than the situation.

Over the following years, I would be tried and tested repeatedly. And sure enough, life has a shared set of problems for everyone in some way or another. January 2018 started beautifully, and by the end of the month, most things were going my way. How could I ask for more?

I felt secure enough to contemplate taking a career break to complete my Master's in information systems management. By mid-February, I forgot I had initiated a paternal test in January to ascertain if I was the child's biological father. Later that month, I got the paternal test results, and of course, I was not the child's biological father at all. I felt exploited, and again, I was easily tripped up. I was annoyed and disappointed with my family, self, and life in general.

The desire to self-medicate and smoke away my troubles came rushing through my veins. I had no plans to quit life this time, but on the other hand, it was a challenge to remain present. Life started to feel like one big ole struggle, but I pressed forward and dealt with my challenges as best as possible.

I had an opportunity to give up my job of eight years and focus on my studies. Without a second thought, I seized the opportunity in April 2018. To some extent, life seems to be going well, or you could say I was "winging it," or rather doing my best to save face. In any case, I was coping and not a bother to anyone. Everything should be fine, but do we get to choose what life throws at us?

As 2018 continued, I lost some friends: my eldest sister in Jamaica and two close friends in Cork who decided to check out on life. And not to mention, around the same time frame, a family friend conned me into handing over €6,500 for a car I would never behold. I directed my hurt toward God and self and felt I had enough. But guess what? Life was not through with me yet.

In January 2019, another friend also surrendered his life. This time, I thought, Aha! I see where this is all going. God is pushing me now beyond my ability to cope. But who am I to make such an impertinent assertion? I am just a man. Since my circumstances are not escaping, I must ask for the strength and courage to ride out my storms.

So, I said, Almighty God, if I must overcome these challenges, please give me patience and the strength to face them. But, still, that old familiar anxiety within started to poke at my core once more.

For months, I focused on my pain and hurt. I reflected on the loss of my eldest sister. I summed up the number of close friends lost, not to mention my wonderful niece (Chevelle Morris) of age 21 (a gentle and caring soul) who was fatally gunned down in Kingston, Jamaica, as she was making her way from a friend's home on 8 January 2010. Boy, wasn't she such a "sweetheart?"

Even as a little child, she had this loving and gentle way about her. She was the "Apple of One's Eyes". Her passing had rocked the entire community, her extended family, and her close relatives. How I wished back then only I were there to save her as I did once before when she was just about 5-6 years of age, but the game of life doesn't always play in one's favour.

Still, while in silence, I was trying to get used to being ripped off €6,500. My thoughts ran amok, and feeling victimised, a sense of responsibility became overwhelmingly burdensome.

I wrestled with self, but that voice within would not allow me to have my way. Supposing one could say it was time to forgive and accept my hurt. I was fighting a battle I could not win. Probably, this would be a good time to forget my two old friends, "Pride and Ego." You see, when the chips are down, and you recognise you can no longer do things on your own or continue in the same manner you have been doing for how long, you must make that bold decision and get off your high horse and seek all the support you can get. At last, my realisation had hit home.

Admittedly, it was not easy to open up and share my pain and suffering with a stranger initially. However, I knew full well that my approach to solving my problems wasn't working for me. But then, as I was to learn, sometimes even a grown man must be honest with himself. I sought help and was amazed to see how many people were willing to provide support. Indeed, all this while I was getting in my way, and over time, I had become an obstacle to self.

Life is undoubtedly one of our most influential tutors, and it has taught me that we should never give up or back down, no matter the circumstance. Quite often, the things that appear so overwhelming today suddenly tomorrow become trivial. Ultimately, it boils down to how One decides to pull Self when times get tough.

Whatever challenges may come your way, remember that someone before you and I had probably been through something similar and survived to tell their story. For the most part, many experiences I have had in Jamaica, in London, and since migrating to Ireland made me stronger and helped me become the man I am today.

Having great role models in our lives will undoubtedly influence the outcomes of life. Likewise, I discovered that I had developed some fundamental coping skills over the years and come to think of it; I owe it to my mother. She was a loyal servant of God, a caring mother who was incredibly patient and forgiving.

Oh man, that woman had some fierce, tenacious attitudes toward life. She was the family's breadwinner, the bedrock, and a determined soul! She was our choir mistress, a baker, and a farmer, but little did I know that in less than two years, Mother was nearing the end of her time given to serve others and her supreme creator. Retrospectively, I thank God I had spent most of my childhood years running around her feet. Who would have thought that everything I learned from her as a child would be vital to support me in my later years? Who would have known that, at the time, she was instilling in me the tools I would desperately need to find my way through life's maze? She was and had been the woman and man of the house. As for my Dad, God bless his soul. He was just the man I grew up to know as my father.

Recently, I have learned not to be dismayed when faced with a challenge because sometimes the things we view as obstacles or hurdles are actual bridges and stepping stones vital to help us along life's journey. Going through hardships sometimes is not bad because we learn so much through experiencing difficult situations. So, as time passes, I realize that some harsh realities of life and misfortunes can bring us better outcomes.

Despite all life's trials and tribulations, setbacks, highs, and lows, I was determined to stay focused. I have achieved a significant milestone by completing my Master's degree as of September 2020 (with Roehampton University in London, UK) and am still holding firm regardless. And speaking of the year 2020: - without a shadow of a doubt, 2020 has been one of the most challenging years for many, if not for every living man on the planet, probably since World War 2, as my mother would argue.

It was a year and time for us to self-reflect and pay close attention to our values, principles, and how we do things in general. It was also a time when many discovered hidden strengths and untapped potentials deep "within" to self-develop and helped others develop themselves and get through the highs and lows of life.

Whether we succumb to life's challenges or rise above them, one thing for sure is that we must all dance to "its beats" and anticipate transformation from our experiences. We must be purposefully committed to "self" and incorporate specific "attitudes and values" into our lives that may impact and improve others' lives.

Your vision of what you desire to create is vital to self-development, growth, and self-worth. Thus, overcoming obstacles must be one's ultimate concern. Remember, though; one cannot have a life free of adversities or disappointments, so we learn to appreciate everything life presents (the good and evil, the high and low) and believe every ounce of trial or tribulation has its purpose.

Once we grasp this, we begin to see that the occurrences of misfortunes aren't set in stone. We start to believe that you, me, or anyone else are blessed to be part of the grand scheme of life and that we live in a world in which we can overcome, defeat, surmount, and cope with whatever life flung our way. Moreover, we possess a deep sense of self-worth and purposefulness.

In the same breath, we should accept that we can positively affect and influence our lives and the lives of others wherever or whenever possible. So, embrace your adversities, challenges, change in circumstance, and keep pressing forward. Ultimately, your story, her story, and his or my story may help someone along their journey.

Tomorrow is a new day, so rise and start anew. Forgive yourself and others, and be forever grateful for your existence. Have no regrets, and don't forget to be thankful for everything; remember, even a man's Prison can become his Palace over time.

"Sometimes out of your biggest misery, comes your greatest gain."
   – Steve Harvey

CHAPTER ELEVEN

YES, YOU WILL MAKE IT TO THE OTHER SIDE

by Angela Russell Grier

I was in foster care until I was adopted a month after I was a year old. Throughout my upbringing, there were many moments when my mother seemed emotionally distant; it made me feel unwanted, like a burden. I am sure she didn't mean to, and I also understand she was a product of her childhood through the Great Depression.

Fortunately, my father, who had experienced the hardships of orphanhood himself in the streets of London, UK, provided me with the warmth and affection I needed. Our shared experience of being orphaned forged a profound bond, bringing us closer together. My father shared his charity work with me when I was five. One was a camp for unserved children that, as a veteran, he started with other vets for children who lost their fathers during WWII.

As a young child, I recall the unsettling moments when my mother's discontentment would manifest in an eerie form of silent indifference. It was a chilling experience, as her silent treatment evoked a profound sense of finality that left me feeling utterly alone. In those heart-wrenching instances, no amount of pleading or desperate apologies could penetrate the wall of her detachment.

I would find myself clutching tightly onto my faithful companion, a pillow named Suzy, as I grappled with a relentless swirl of anxiety and uncertainty. The fear of being "sent back" loomed over me, hauntingly magnified by the fact that I did not even know where this "back" was. A complex and profound form of fear etched its mark upon my spirit, shaping my understanding of abandonment and the fragile nature of our sense of belonging.

At nine, my life took a dramatic turn when my father suffered a stroke. The one person I truly felt safe with was no more, and more dysfunction loomed on the horizon. My parents had endured the hardships of the Great Depression, and my father had served as a medic on the front lines of WWII.

Tragically, they had lost two children as stillborn at birth, as the RH negative factor had not yet been discovered, hence how I entered the picture. Due to my father's immobility, we moved to a single-level house. In our town, most women did not drive, which unfortunately meant my mother lost her support system.

Within a year, my father had a second stroke that immobilized him; losing his job at only 49 years old and controlling his body and mind was highly challenging as someone who had always been a problem solver and advocate for those in need. Soon, his fellow veteran buddies would visit, always bringing alcohol. Within a short period, he began drinking daily. My mother, trapped in the house, eventually joined him. My once strict Catholic parents had become completely dysfunctional.

By age ten, the roles had reversed: I was now caring for my parents while trying to conceal our family secret, burdened by immense shame. One month after turning fifteen, I tragically discovered my mother's lifeless body on the kitchen floor; she had died of a massive coronary. Within seventeen months,

I had experienced the heartbreak of burying my parents and grandparents and found myself completely alone. No adult came to rescue me, so I had to figure out how to save myself.

The pain of staying in my hometown became unbearable. This prompted a desperate need to break free. I fled Canada, seeking solace in the United Kingdom, hoping to start anew while leaving the pain behind. But of course, as we mature, we know we can't run away from pain. We need to turn and face the pain and rescue ourselves.

While searching for where to run, I unknowingly stumbled upon a Catholic Grammar school. Little did I know how strictly the group of nuns ran this place. You would've thought I should have known better. Starting in Kindergarten, I quickly earned the reputation of being that kid who couldn't resist questioning the logic behind the stories and teachings of Catholicism. The nuns didn't take kindly to my inquisitive nature, and I became well acquainted with the yardstick, the pointer, and even the dreaded black leather strap. I was always on the receiving end of their disciplinary measures.

However, in desperation for a roof over my head, three square meals a day must have clouded my judgment when I enrolled here. The contradictions, the mysteries, the blind faith required—it was all too much for my questioning mind to handle. Truthfully, my religion went AWOL at the ripe old age of fourteen. For the next six months, I stealthily navigated the strict rules and sky-high expectations as I meticulously planned my grand getaway from the clutches of the convent school. My mission was to break free from the chains that bound me to a belief system I no longer believed in. In hindsight, my involuntary enrolment was both a comical mishap and a challenging adventure.

I finally wrangled my way out – I was free! There was only one tiny problem: As the large black iron gates closed behind me, I was left without a place to rest my rebellious head. A month before my sixteenth birthday, I sofa-surfed and even tested my survival skills' limits by spending a week camping out in Hyde Park. Many leftover hippies were there, so I felt like I was on an adventure. Luckily, fate smiled upon me, and there was a washroom nearby. For just 10 pence, I could wash each morning and face the world as a clean, respectable individual.

Interestingly, I had no idea I was homeless until I was fifty-four. By this time, I was working in the nonprofit sector and writing my fifth grant to procure funding for unhoused children. Realisation dawned after writing the exact words in each grant – as my brain shouted, 'Hey, wait a minute, I was homeless and didn't know it!' Homelessness had a different connotation back then.

This was just the beginning of many more chapters that dealt with *Ignorance* mixed with a heap of *Hope* for youth. I spent a transformative span between the ages of 15 and 22, embarking on a whirlwind journey that led me to reside in six different countries. I found that the charity work my father had involved me, starting as a small child, opened my eyes to the struggles and hardships faced by others. It taught me the value of empathy, compassion, and gratitude. And so, every day, no matter how small, I sought to find something to be grateful for. It was a practice that kept my spirit grounded and my heart open.

In moments of doubt or uncertainty, I would return to the story of Pandora's Box, a tale that had stayed with me since fifth grade. I remembered how all the uglies had been released, causing chaos and despair. But out of the darkness emerged *Hope*, the gentle force that brought light and possibility. That story became a constant reminder that even in the face of adversity, there is always a glimmer of *Hope,* a chance for something better.

Driven by an unyielding thirst for knowledge, I pursued my education wherever the opportunity presented itself, seizing every chance to expand my horizons in a nomadic pursuit of intellectual growth.

I went through a devastating marriage from 27 to 30 – I finally divorced – but it is too much to go into here. Suffice it to say that I got through that and became more resilient. By age thirty, I was living in the United States, and destiny had an interesting twist awaiting me. Against all odds, I uncovered the elusive truth of my origin and met my birth parents. Astonishingly, they had come together twenty-five years after my birth and were now married. I wish I could say that the reunion was as blissful as those we see on TV, with skies parting and angels singing in harmonious celebration. But the truth is, it wasn't. There were no dramatic flourishes or cinematic moments. However, amid it all, I discovered something more significant than grand gestures or theatrical reunions. I found a missing piece of myself, a revelation that clarified my existence. I had always felt a sizeable, gaping hole within me - a missing puzzle piece that seemed insurmountable. But as I stood face to face with my biological parents, I realised this missing piece wasn't as overwhelming as I had imagined. A fraction of 10% of the complete picture made me who I am.

At that moment, I understood that I was more than the sum of my genetics. I was my own person, distinct from my parents in so many ways. Yes, I finally resembled someone, and some of my quirks had an explanation. I could trace the threads of ancestry and medical history that weaved into my being.

But in the eternal debate of nature versus nurture, it became clear that the nurture provided by my adoptive father, my "real father," the man who raised me until I was nine, had ultimately shaped my character and despite the brevity of our time together, those formative years laid the foundation for my aspirations and my relentless pursuit of personal growth. They instilled in me the drive to reach higher, regardless of the obstacles thrown my way.

Looking back, I couldn't help but feel an overwhelming sense of gratitude. I am grateful for the brief but impactful presence of the parents who raised me. Their love and even the tribulations during those eight short years helped mould me into the determined individual I am today.

I understood that my journey would have taken a drastically different turn had my birth mother chosen a different path. Realising this truth only deepened my appreciation for the experiences I had been granted.

Life has an uncanny way of leading us down unexpected paths and teaching us invaluable lessons. Though not a fairy tale, this reunion gave me a sense of identity and a newfound understanding of my story. It reminded me of embracing the past while forging my destiny.

For some reason, life led me to reconnect with my birth parents, albeit briefly, long enough to walk alongside them as they transitioned to another life beyond this one. I had only met my biological father once.

I then unexpectedly found myself in a different country, managing the hospital and doctors on his behalf, as my birth mother was too distraught. Similarly, several years later, I found myself in a similar situation with my birth mother, which, at this point, I had only met three times prior.

Eight years later, after meeting my birth parents, I again found love and remarried. My husband and I built a life together and became business partners, driven by our ambition and desire for success. Amid it all, the idea of starting a family had been put on hold. Time seemed to slip away, and at 43, we realised that our window of opportunity was closing.

It was as if the Universe sensed our longing and decided to bring balance to our lives. As soon as we decided to embark on the journey of parenthood, a miracle occurred. To our surprise, I became pregnant without needing medical intervention. At 44, I gave birth to our beautiful and healthy daughter. The doctors marvelled at this incredible feat, recognising the rarity of such a successful pregnancy without any previous children my age. Our daughter was unquestionably a miracle, a gift from above that we were meant to cherish. From 43 to 49, I experienced pure bliss for the next six years. My heart was filled with indescribable joy and fulfillment. However, life throws unexpected curveballs, and our happiness soon turns into a tumultuous journey.

It all began with a change in my husband's personality, followed by haunting hallucinations. The sudden and rapid shifts lasted only half an hour to an hour. Filled with worry, I relentlessly sought help, taking him from one doctor to another. But our plea for assistance fell on deaf ears. His symptoms were dismissed and labelled as depression and alcoholism. He was prescribed various medications for his mental health condition, worsening the situation.

Deep down, I sensed something more at play, something much more severe than what was initially diagnosed. I feared my husband might be battling early-onset Alzheimer's or another form of dementia. The medical professionals had misjudged his condition, only to discover that he was fighting a battle against cancer. The protein consumption caused his ammonia and bilirubin levels to spike, leading to bouts of drunken behaviour that lasted for a mere hour.

This sudden twist in our lives was devastating. The man I loved, my partner in life and business, was now confronted with a life-threatening illness. We navigated the treacherous cancer path together, clinging to hope and fighting against the odds. The once vibrant and spirited man had become a shadow of his former self, his body ravaged by the relentless disease.

I became his caregiver, shouldering the weight of his physical and emotional pain. Life had once again hit an unexpected storm. He died six days after our daughter turned nine; ironically, her life changed significantly at the same age as it did for me.

Now, at the age of 53, without my husband as my business partner, I had to shut down our business, and once again, I found I needed to reinvent myself and start over again. I threw myself into the nonprofit sector, which was very cathartic. As my father did for me, I introduced my daughter to some of my nonprofit work, which has been cathartic for her and taught her the value of empathy, compassion, and gratitude.

My daughter was in her second-to-last year of high school when the COVID-19 pandemic hit. We were housebound, just like the rest of the world. While she worked on finishing high school in her room, I decided, at 60, to work alongside her and pursue my MBA, which I am about to complete. As a glutton for punishment, I plan on pursuing another Master's degree as soon as this ends, intending to support others through counselling. I hope sharing my story will encourage and support you as you navigate your challenges.

I want to share a trick I used while going through some of my darkest times. I would pretend I was the director of my movie, and when parts caused despair or anxiety, I would imagine yelling "CUT" and rewriting how I wanted the film to go. This helped me immensely, especially during sleepless nights. So, as I rewrote my story in my mind's eye, I would find myself drifting off to sleep. And you know what was truly impressive about this exercise? I discovered I was manifesting many things I had rewritten in my life script!

As the chapters of my life unfolded, I encountered both triumphs and challenges. There were moments of immense joy, fulfillment, severe heartache, and uncertainty when the storm clouds seemed to gather overhead. But through it all, I held onto the flickering flame of *Hope*, knowing that it would guide me through the darkest times.

As I reflect upon those transformative years, I am grateful for the journey I undertook. The whirlwind of experiences, the diverse landscapes, and the incredible people I met along the way have shaped me into who I am today. I carry the lessons of gratitude and *Hope* within me, embedding them deep into the core of my being. They remind me to be grateful for the present moment, cherish the beauty surrounding me, and embrace the unknown chapters that lie ahead.

As my story unfolds, each page brings new adventures and opportunities. And as I turn the pages, I do so with a heart filled with hope and a spirit ready to embrace whatever comes my way, for I know that despite the twists and turns, the ups and downs, there will always be hope, shining its light and reminding me that every chapter holds the potential for a heartfelt story.

CHAPTER TWELVE

"Do not judge me by my success, judge me by how many times I fell and returned." - Nelson Mandela

RESILIENCE: THE KEY TO UNLOCKING YOUR POTENTIAL

by Dr. Angeliki Papasava

In today's fast-paced and unpredictable world, resilience has emerged as a critical attribute for individuals, teams, and organisations. Adapting, persevering, and thriving in adversity and uncertainty are valuable and often essential for success. Resilience encompasses resourcefulness, mental and emotional strength, and the capacity to bounce back from setbacks more robustly than before.

Demonstrating remarkable resilience refers to the ability or capacity of an individual, system, or community to withstand, recover from, or adapt to challenging or stressful conditions. It is the ability to bounce back or recover quickly from difficulties, failures, or adverse circumstances, adapt, and thrive in adversity, demonstrating emotional and psychological strength in challenging circumstances. It's a process that involves a combined approach of psychological, emotional, social, and physical factors that allow individuals or systems to confront and navigate through difficult situations, such as trauma, losses, failures, or significant life changes.

It is not about avoiding or eliminating challenges but developing inner strength, flexibility, and adaptive skills necessary to respond and cope with adversity effectively. It also includes having a positive mindset, maintaining a sense of hope, and identifying and utilising available resources and support networks. It's a dynamic process that can be cultivated and strengthened through various strategies, including building supportive relationships, practicing self-care, developing problem-solving skills, fostering optimism, and learning from past experiences.

Research has shown that resilience is influenced by various protective factors, such as self-efficacy, an optimistic attitude, a social support mechanism, a sense of purpose, appropriate coping skills, and the ability to face and overcome adversity. These protective factors can enhance strength and promote positive adaptation when dealing with difficult situations.

Let's consider self-efficacy, which refers to an individual's belief in their ability to cope with challenges and difficulties successfully. Individuals with a strong sense of self-efficacy are more likely to approach difficult situations with confidence, perseverance, and problem-solving skills, thus enhancing their resilience. Optimistic individuals tend to view setbacks as temporary and surmountable, have faith in their ability to face challenges and maintain hope for the future. Similarly, having a reliable, supportive network of family, friends, and other relationships becomes a critical protective factor. Social solid connections provide emotional support, practical assistance, and a sense of belonging, which can help individuals better cope with stress and adversity.

When individuals have clear goals, self-values, and a sense of purpose or direction, they are more likely to persevere and find true meaning in harsh conditions. Practical coping skills and strategies are significant factors in the dynamic process of becoming resilient. These may include problem-solving skills, emotion regulation techniques, stress management strategies, and adaptive coping mechanisms.

Developing and utilising healthy coping skills can help individuals navigate adversity and maintain their well-being. Similarly, having a positive and beneficial healthy relationship provides a sense of trust, stability, and emotional security, which can counterbalance the adverse effects of stress and protect strength. Recognising, understanding, and managing emotions effectively can help individuals navigate challenging situations, maintain emotional well-being, and adapt to adversity. These protective factors are not exhaustive; nevertheless, they highlight some crucial aspects that can contribute to resilience in individuals.

Being resilient involves some forms of adaptability and the capacity to adjust to new circumstances or challenging situations. It is not about rigidly maintaining the status quo but instead developing the ability to bounce back from adversity, support well-being, adapt to changes, and thrive in response to new circumstances or demands. Moreover, it is a process that involves recovering and regaining stability after experiencing setbacks, stress, or difficult situations. It consists of effectively coping with adversity, maintaining a positive mindset, and utilising available resources and support systems. Suffice it to say individuals often considered resilient demonstrate flexibility, perseverance, and a willingness to learn from their experiences.

On the contrary, adaptability focuses on the ability to adjust one's thoughts, behaviours, and strategies in response to changing circumstances. It involves being open to new ideas, being able to think creatively, and being willing to embrace and navigate through uncertainty. Adaptable individuals can quickly assess situations, identify necessary changes, and respond effectively to new challenges. By all accounts, you could say resilience and adaptability complement each other.

Conversely, stability provides a foundation for individuals to withstand and recover from adversity, while adaptability enables individuals to navigate through changing environments or situations proactively and successfully. Together, they contribute to an individual's ability to thrive and grow in the face of challenges, uncertainty, and change. Developing resilience, adaptability, and a stable mindset can lead to more significant personal growth, improved problem-solving skills, and increased well-being.

Resilient individuals adjust and adapt to new circumstances, enabling them to navigate challenges and maintain their well-being effectively. So, rather than rigidly clinging to the status quo or resisting change, resilient individuals are open to exploring new strategies, perspectives, and solutions. In the face of adversity, resilient individuals are willing to reassess their approach, make necessary adjustments, and seek alternative paths. They recognise that what may have worked in the past might not be applicable in the current situation and are willing to explore innovative solutions. This flexibility and adaptability allow them to find new ways to overcome obstacles and move forward.

Adaptability in resilience also involves being open-minded and receptive to feedback and learning opportunities. Thus, it is essential to develop an open mindset and willingness to consider different viewpoints, seek advice and support from others, and continuously learn and grow from your experiences to change, evolve, and embrace the opportunities for personal and professional development that may arise from challenging situations. Consequently, your moral responsibility is to foster the capacity to effectively navigate adversity when combining adaptability with other protective factors like perseverance, problem-solving skills, and social support.

Inarguably, difficult situations can provide opportunities for personal growth, self-reflection, and learning, extracting invaluable lessons from your experiences and applying them to plan for or circumnavigate future challenges. This self-reflection enables you to identify areas for improvement, adjust your approaches, and develop effective coping strategies for future adversities.

Safe to say, when confronted with challenging situations, you are presented with growth opportunities, or you could allow your dire situation to become your shackles, or you could exploit and rise above your challenging circumstances, get out of your comfort zone, develop new skills, cultivate strength, and discover inner resources you may never fathom you possess.

In short, you might gain a deeper understanding of your abilities and true potential by conquering adversity. Furthermore, resilient individuals approach challenges with a growth mindset. They view setbacks and failures as opportunities for learning and improvement rather than as indications of personal inadequacy. This mindset allows them to persevere, bounce back, and adapt to future challenges more effectively.

The process of growth and learning in resilience is not limited to individual development. It can also extend to interpersonal relationships and community resilience. Through a shared understanding of adversities, people and communities can learn from each other, foster empathy, and performance, and collectively build strength. Overall, resilience is not just about enduring hardship but also about harnessing the potential for growth and learning that adversity presents. By embracing these opportunities, resilient individuals develop greater self-awareness, acquire new skills, and cultivate the mindset and tools to navigate future challenges successfully.

Intrinsically, resilience holds immense importance in various aspects of life, particularly in the professional realm. Resilient individuals face challenges head-on, maintain a positive mindset, and adapt to changing circumstances. They exhibit perseverance, optimism, flexibility, and emotional intelligence, enabling them to navigate obstacles and setbacks effectively.

The impact of resilience extends beyond personal well-being. Resilient individuals are more productive, innovative, and capable of overcoming obstacles. They are better equipped to handle stress, manage conflicts, and maintain high personal and professional engagement levels. They focus on developing emotional regulation, problem-solving, adaptability, and self-care skills to cultivate resilience. As we continue to navigate an ever-changing and unpredictable world, the importance of stability becomes even more evident. By embracing strength at a personal and professional level, we can survive and prosper in the face of challenges, fostering personal and professional growth.

CHAPTER THIRTEEN

FROM DESPAIR TO AN AUTHENTIC AND AMAZING LIFE

by Julie Bagley

This chapter is the final story in our book about overcoming and becoming. It encompasses topics including suicide and depression but is essentially a story of resilience, authenticity, and hope.

Craig and I had known each other for around 20 years before we got together. We'd been in a musical called Calamity Jane, back in 1994. I was Calamity, and he was Bill Hickock. We were great friends and married then, so we didn't think anything further about it. When we got together 20 years later, he was divorced, and I was separated. I'd known he had experienced a tough upbringing by his father. Being the eldest of four and feeling unloved created significant mental anguish. He was also a cancer survivor and had other health challenges which affected his emotional well-being. Little did I know how this combination of health and upbringing problems had affected his mental capacity. Compounding this PTSD trauma, Craig had further physical issues after two failed spinal fusions that resulted in chronic pain. We married in

2012, but the mental and physical pain got progressively worse.

Craig was taking oxycodone for the pain. Research has advised it is not the best option for chronic pain and is known to cause some patients to go down a dark path[1]. Craig was on this path and, in June 2018, committed suicide. Craig didn't leave a note; he threatened a lot in the previous 2½ years, detailing how he'd end his own life. He was emotionally abusive, reflecting his father's approach he'd endured. I did what I could to support him. At the same time, I prepared myself should he ever follow through. Unfortunately, my 19-year-old daughter found him. The day he died, I had gone home from work to check on him at lunchtime; he seemed OK, so I headed back to work.

Craig was a brilliant man, a podiatrist, musician, and actor who loved the arts. At his wake, I found that he had told some friends that the cancer had returned and was deeply anxious and troubled. It was his reality and meaning-making of what was happening, compounded by the chronic pain and the wrong medication prescribed for it. We lost a shining light with an uncontrolled flickering that day, yet I was relieved to be out of the continual cycle of worry, of wondering if he was going to be alive when I got home. It was traumatising and a relief at the same time.

What happened after that had the biggest impact. The shock when someone dies at one's hand and the unexpected timing is hard enough but put in the mix your 19-year-old daughter, who was two weeks out from exams, finding him. She did her exams and passed, but the event filled her with long-lasting trauma. Considerable counselling has helped; she now resides in the UK, teaching and working as a musician. Craig's suicide left me with nothing; I couldn't even pay the rent. Becoming homeless was a real possibility.

I'd taken a Landmark Forum[2] six weeks before; unbeknownst to me then, it would give me the focus needed to move through the adversity I faced. The Landmark Forum is a program designed to bring about positive and permanent shifts in the quality of one's life. The Landmark forum gave me the tools and tenacity to be present and in the now whilst grieving, yet at the same time, I wanted to sit in the corner and hide from the world. The Landmark growth and development program helped me to accept the grief, acknowledge it was Craig's choice, that I had done everything to support him, and not be engulfed by guilt but just sadness. I had to admit that he chose his path. He would always say to everyone, 'Make your life amazing.' After that, I took from the event and sought to 'make my life amazing' in honour of Craig and the good times we had together, for myself and for my two daughters. I had to reflect on myself, how I was dealing with the events and how to move forward.

I chose to rise above it. I have two beautiful grown-up daughters I want to show I could. I tried to find out what I stand for to make my mark on the world. I wanted to be there for them. Show them that you can survive adversity. But it takes looking at yourself and doing something different.

I didn't want people to rescue me; I needed to make my opportunities. I didn't fit into the neat boxes culturally, where there is a view that women fit into this or that box. Australia had stopped the widow pension, so I had to find suitable work within two weeks or be homeless. Some people aren't nice; I experienced a narcissistic boss who was unsympathetic to my plight. I had to seek work; I was being the brunt of her negativity that this event compounded. I didn't want to deal with the language she bombarded me with. I didn't want to be bitter like she was, so I moved on. It was a hard choice moving on from a wage but I needed to for my wellbeing.

I wanted to make a mark in the world and have the capacity to do something worthy, be a role model. I wanted to honour Craig and make my life amazing. So, I moved to Canberra, looking for work. There, I met John. It wasn't expected. I was on a journey of self-discovery and self-reflection at the time. I was looking for who I am and what I can offer to help others through trauma. At the same time, I was looking for what I could do to ensure I could be OK financially while I kept doing my growth and development program.

Having never studied, I wanted to go to university. When I came across the interesting Ducere MBA, I was reaching out to several universities, so I wrote off for the brochure. Ducere rang with 24 hours, I talked through my story and said I did the growth and development forum to show I could commit to studying. To my surprise, the person on the other phone had done the same program. I was accepted with a scholarship for the MBA. I considered it a gift, meant to be my next step. I love every minute of my MBA and can't wait to finish and live what I've learned. I want to help others to live a life that gives fulfilment. Contributing to work, family, kids, colleagues at work, and university all light me up to see others doing something that fills them with joy. I'm working towards a business in coaching, using an inquiry base and curiosity to co-create[3] a joy-filled life.

I want to avoid getting lost in the seriousness of life. I remember my mentor in life; she was elegant and my dance teacher as I worked to become a professional dancer. She died in the UK from motor neuron disease in 2006. I learned so much confidence from her. We ran a charity concert in 2008. I danced and sang, and we raised £50K to contribute to motor neuron research in the UK. It is something I am proud of, being able to contribute toward the much-needed research, it is this joy I want to feel again.

Cancer and disease can be hideous, the seen and unseen. I've gone through losing my Dad to an aortic aneurysm after having survived cancer just six months before Craig's suicide in 2018. Dad was in the UK and I was in Australia, having been a professional dancer, I'd had spinal surgery six years earlier and had a relapse so couldn't fly to be with Dad or attend his funeral. I haven't been back to the UK since 2015. Since then, a friend's husband died from brain cancer with twins only three years old. Watching her cope and how she is bringing up two children on her own has been amazing. Through it all, she has shown me that you can have control and choose to be happy.

My advice is to honour the memory of the person who has passed AND make something of your life as well. You want the best for your kids and your partner; let love thrive. It would be a disservice to mope around and use it as an excuse not to live a great life. I chose to invest in myself and not wait for others to fix and change things. I had family in the UK, the love of good friends, and grown kids, but no money to bail me out. I needed to develop and grow, and my network of friends made a difference. I didn't hide it or try to be perfect. I was authentic in my grief and my anger, and I was open to others contributing to my evolution and self-reflection. We are social constructs of being an organism; if we don't share authenticity, we deny others.

Authenticity is the sense of being true to your mind, body, and soul, no matter what life throws at you. Be candid with yourself and others. Your values, beliefs, ideals, and actions will align by practicing kindness and taking responsibility for your actions. ... and yes, life can be amazing.

CONCLUSION

by Warren Dix

In sterquiliniis invenitur– in filth, it will be found. "That which you most need to find will be found where you least want to look."

– Carl Jung

Fundamentally, this book embodies the authors' journey and represents the degree of challenges and adversities they have endured at some point in life, but still managed to transform their obstacles into stepping stones. Throughout this book, the authors have shared the importance of overcoming challenges, obstacles and embracing change and its impact on their lives. Their transformational stories accentuate the characteristics and behaviour and the strategies and techniques essential for overcoming adversity, individual or personal "**change**" which leads us to the essence of this book.

Change is an inevitable part of life, presenting challenges and opportunities for personal and professional growth. Paradoxically, change is complex, and personal transformation is even more difficult. We are regularly confronted with changes in everyday life, work, business, or personal situations.

What is the impact on us as individuals? How do we keep up without losing control or freezing into old ways and missing opportunities for growth? Constant changes around us can appear out of control and be very demotivating. But knowledge is power and knowing that our brains are wired to resist growth and adaptation puts us in a position to embrace change and how we can use it to grow and become better people, partners, friends, or leaders.

These events are not of our choosing. However, we do choose how we respond. Responding with growth or a positive mindset is still within our control.

"Atticus says you can choose your friends, but you sho' can't choose your family, and they're still kin to you whether you acknowledge them or not, and it makes you look silly when you don't".

The quote from Harper Lee's *"To Kill a Mockingbird"* resonates with many people. In families, for better or worse, we experience change. Sometimes minor, sometimes significant. The dynamics within our immediate and extended family further result in change. We are affected by relocation, divorce, and a new family member. Our friends get us into trouble and out of trouble. The changes from these events can be significant or inconsequential.

Regardless of the source of the changes we did not initiate, change inevitably occurs to most of us, and it's up to us to choose how to respond. Change has many faces, sources, reasons, and outcomes that could be useful or detrimental to us. ***Change*** *within* our personal growth defines how well we cope in an ever-changing world! Can we fundamentally change ourselves? Or are we buffeted by the seas of change agents that don't allow us to chart our voyage?

When we do contribute and speak up, and it leads to change, is that not just our contribution to the ocean of change out there? It is, but the question is, where did that come from? What within you decided it was essential to present the change you wanted to see?

How we manage our change in circumstance resulting from external forces has been studied across many disciplines. The most common being psychology, science, philosophy, and sociology. I will throw in leadership literature for good measure. My takeaway is that we respond in one of two ways. We take control of what we can and adapt to the new reality. Or, we believe we have no control and get stuck in an endless spiral of victimization. It is possible to live within this framework, but it's not optimal.

People as individuals and their context in the world - The Kubler-Ross model was initially developed to describe personal loss and grieving stages. The five stages are denial, anger, bargaining, depression, and acceptance. Critics of the model propose that these are states as opposed to stages. Nonetheless, the model is widely referenced and still considered valid. Acceptance ultimately still leads us to how a person responds, "acceptance" suggests leaning towards a positive outcome.

Attributed to Socrates, the dictum "the unexamined life is not worth living" is one of many that hold at its essence that "change" is growth. One may not consciously examine one's life, but those of us tolerate, accept, or embrace change instead of surviving.

For those who are more active or aware of self-reflection, it becomes more meaningful and rewarding to fulfill our destiny by first examining one-self. The examination leads to insights, room for improvement, and (depending on skill and other criteria) leads to correction or change.

What does it then take to be our change agent? Sometimes, we find ourselves in a situation where we did not trigger the change, but we still need to choose how to respond. Suppose you are predisposed to a growth mindset and perceive change to be positive. Chances are good that you will do what is required to adapt to the change, albeit change in finance, job loss, or losing a loved one.

Alternatively, to recognise the need to change without gentle (or not so gentle) nudging. It requires looking within yourself and saying, hey, something needs to change! Introspection leads to a desire for something different. Desire is strong enough to make a conscious effort to change how you see things or to want to understand better how others view the same thing from their perspective. This enables you to take one more step on the ladder of life.

Desire to change is a constant conscious effort that will lead to a rewarding life. That is the elixir of life: learn to (or want to learn to) adapt and understand those around you. How do you adapt? You leverage your awareness and develop a growth mindset to open yourself to becoming better.

The good, the bad and the ugly of modern life - We are drowning in digital information. Educational, informative, entertaining, and downright ludicrous information. Information or data is bombarding us from all sides with text, imagery, tweets, posts, and videos.

Our innate human disposition to compare is suddenly fed an ongoing unrealistic barrage of data on how we should be. This includes many philosophies, psychological and sociological commentary, and tools to improve and become better. Depending on your choices, habits, or the algorithms that have trapped you, one cannot help but compare. Often, these external factors, no matter how well-meaning, are the extrinsic forces that make us want to change.

These drivers can be powerful and effective. Yet, if you go down the wrong internet rabbit hole, you could lose yourself in a warren of risky echo chambers. Fundamentally, change led by yourself will be more effective and rewarding. Done correctly, it would also be more relevant as it would align with your goals, desires, and values. In other words, the best change is that you have identified and want to tweak in yourself.

The avenues to explore or guide you in your new awareness are numerous. Do you visit our favourite social media resource to find the right tools? Do you buy books? These are certainly options available. They might be limited in sustainable change or efficacy as these resources do not cater to you specifically, who you are, what you have been through, or your world vision.

U in unique is you - We are unique in our view of the world. Not even twins raised in the same household can share identical world views. There are just too many parameters that influence our lives. This influence leads us to gain a unique perspective. We are influenced by external elements and genetics, internalised to create a unique being. That unique being needs special tools. Regardless of how motivated, intelligent, and introspective we are, we need a personalized approach and a sounding board to understand actual change.

Simply put, we do not know what we do not know! Or put differently, we are faced with unknown unknowns. If we could upload all the knowledge in the world into our brains, we certainly would know a lot. However, even that premise is impossible because knowledge is not only knowing explicit things. For instance, knowledge includes what your next-door neighbour knows through their experience, and you cannot know that, too. So, how do you translate the '*unknown unknown*' to explicit knowledge? You can't be alone, at any rate. But don't let that discourage you. No one knows the unknown. So, where do you start? Start by sharing.

It would be best to have a sounding board to share your thoughts with, someone who can reflect them to you honestly. Someone who will help you gain a different perspective. If you are open to the process, you will start seeing things in a new light. You will begin to shift from one view to another. You will examine your thoughts, beliefs, and values to understand your thoughts and feelings better.

You will update your ideas and perspectives to align more closely with your values. You will release long-held limiting beliefs and move closer to the person you believe you can be. The person who you know, at the core of your being, you aim to be. You will grow because you have accepted that you need to change. Change your way of thinking, your views, opinions, and thoughts about others.

Who do you use as your sounding board? Who is the saviour that will lead you to personal enlightenment?

You need to be able to trust the person explicitly. It would be best to speak with someone who will not judge you and, by extension, judge how you think. Ideally, that person needs the time and space to be available for you to hold space. They need to be present for you while you are present for them. You do not want advice; you want to be responsible for finding the change required from within yourself. After all, you know yourself better than anyone else.

Interestingly, this person is usually not your partner, sibling, parent, or best friend. They are too close to you, and their view of you has evolved on the same or similar trajectory as your view of yourself. It's difficult for them to be impartial. Who then? A mentor could be a helpful start, especially for career growth.

Mentors should have your best interest at heart, and they should have experience in the area in which you are looking to grow. An experienced mentor can be priceless. Religious leaders are good resources to tap into, especially for personal growth. A good therapist will be a choice if you need to resolve issues in your past, deal with trauma, etc.

However, if you are just 'stuck,' you are looking for a skilled coach to enable you to grow. Someone who will partner with you to overcome your limiting beliefs, objections, or constraints. To demonstrate all the requirements set out above. People trained as coaches, be that a life coach, executive coach, transformation coach, etc., are a valuable resource to find for sustainable personal growth.

"Change will not come if we wait for some other person or some other time. We are the ones we've been waiting for. We are the change that we seek."
　– Barack Obama

We have learned that our brains are naturally resistant to change but capable of adapting and evolving. By understanding our mindset and being open to new possibilities, we can overcome the fear and resistance often accompanying change, becoming ever more resilient.

As individuals, we must identify our blind spots and areas where we can improve. This self-awareness allows us to break free from old patterns and habits that may be holding us back from becoming the best versions of ourselves. Whether in our careers, relationships, or personal development, there are always opportunities for growth and positive change. Recognising the different responses to change is essential for leaders. Understanding their perspectives using coaching techniques and providing support can make implementing complex changes smoother and more successful.

Undoubtedly, living life to its fullest has its own challenges, but we pray that now you have finished reading this beautiful piece, you will be empowered to discover your true power, becoming resilient, adaptable, and make meaningful changes to circumvent the harsh realities of life.

In addition to this, it is helpful to remember that what you most need to find will be found where you least want to look. That takes courage. Let those who have moved on from past experiences not re-live them as you try to find your place in this world, so I hope this helps you to embrace change and view your obstacles as opportunities to self-develop, be open to learning, and take proactive steps toward accomplishing your dreams and goals.

REFERENCES

Following are references by chapter as provided by the author.

Chapter 2

[1] Weller, M. (1992) The International Response to the Dissolution of the Socialist Federal Republic of Yugoslavia. *American Journal of International Law*, 86(3), pp.569-607. doi:10.2307/2203972

[2] Kandeva, E. (ed.) (2001) *Stabiliziation of Local Governments. Local Government and Public Service Reform Initiative.* Budapest, Hungary: Open Society Institute. http://pdc.ceu.hu/archive/00006992/01/LGI_Stabilizatio n-of-Local-Governments_2001.pdf#page=417

[3] Korhan, A.R.U.N. (2014) Kosovo force (kfor) organization image: empirical research on Kosovo Security Forces (KSF). *Dokuz Eylül Üniversitesi Sosyal Bilimler Enstitüsü Dergisi*, 16(4), pp.537-558. https://dergipark.org.tr/ en/download/article-file/53259

[4] Kolankiewicz, G. (2000) Towards a sociology of the transition: rights, resources and social integration in Poland (Vol. 48). *UCL School of Slavonic and East European Studies* (SSEES). https://discovery.ucl.ac.uk/id/eprint/24830/ 2/SSEES0031.pdf

[5] Strohmeyer, H. (2001) Collapse and Reconstruction of ajudicial System: The United Nations Missions in Kosovo and East Timor. *American Journal of International Law,* 95(1), pp.46-63. https://biblioteca.cejamericas.org/bi tstream/handle/2015/1509/collapse-onu-east-timor.pdf?sequence=1&isAll owed=y

[6] Pickering, P.M., 2010. Assessing international aid for local governance in the Western Balkans. Democratization, 17(5), pp.1024-1049. https://peopl

e.wm.edu/~pmpick/research/PickeringDemocratizationPublished.pdf

Chapter Four

[1] van der Westhuizen, B. (2004) On the wings of a story by Aggrey of Africa: Fly, Eagle, Fly!. *Journal of African Children's and Youth Literature*, 15, pp.27-38. https://go.gale.com/ps/i.do?id=GALE%7CA192351979&sid=googleScholar& v=2.1&it=r&linkaccess=abs&issn=&p=AONE&sw=w&userGroupName=anon %7E39db71c4&aty=open-web-entry

Chapter Six

[1] Horniman, A. (2013) Leadership and Choice Theory. *Darden Case No. UVA-OB-1052*, Available at SSRN: https://ssrn.com/abstract=2974828 or http://dx .doi.org/10.2139/ssrn.2974828

[2] Julian. L. (2002) *God is my CEP: Following God's principles in a bottom-line world*. Adams Media Group.

[3] Sanborn. M. (2005) *The Fred Factor*. Century Trade.

[4] Maxwell, J. C. (2001) *Developing the Leader Within You*. Thomas Nelson US.

[5] Stanley A. (2004) *The Best Ever: learning to foolproof your life.* Multnomah Press.

[6] Martin Luther King Jr > Quotes > Quotable Quotes. https://www.goodre ads.com/author/quotes/23924.Martin_Luther_King_Jr_

[7] Guest, E.A. (1922). Myself. *The Journal of Education*, 96(5 (2391), pp.123-123.

Chapter Nine

[1] Wim Hof Method (2023) *Effects of the Wim Hof Method on your autoimmune nervous system.* https://www.wimhofmethod.com/controlling-the-autono mic-nervous-system#:~:text=With%20consistent%20practice%2C%20it %20is,and%20overall%20improved%20well%2Dbeing.

[2] GSMA (2012) *Annual Report 2012* https://www.gsma.com/mobilefordev elopment/wp-content/uploads/2012/10/2012_MMU_Annual-Report.pdf

[3] U.S. Embassy in Malawi (2017) Government Announcement , *Gov.scot*

https://www.gov.scot/binaries/content/documents/govscot/publications/foi-eir-release/2017/12/foi-17-02791/documents/foi-17-02791-annex-p-email-correspondence-pdf/foi-17-02791-annex-p-email-correspondence-pdf/govscot:document/FOI-17-02791-Annex%20A-P%20Email%20Correspondence.pdf

[4] Eckhard Störmer, E., Bontoux, L., Krzysztofowicz, M., Florescu, E., Bock, A., and Scapolo, F. (2020) Chapter 12 - Foresight – Using Science and Evidence to Anticipate and Shape the Future in: Šucha, V. and Sienkiewicz, M. (Eds.) *Science for Policy Handbook*, Elsevier.

[5] Margolis,J. D. and Stoltz, P. (2010) How to Bounce Back from Adversity, *Harvard Business Review* (Jan-Feb, 2010)

Chapter Thirteen

[1] Leung, J., Santo, T., Colledge-Frisby, S., Mekonen, T., Thomson, K., Degenhardt, L., Connor, J. P., Hall, W., Stjepanović, D. (2022) Mood and Anxiety Symptoms in Persons Taking Prescription Opioids: A Systematic Review with Meta-Analyses of Longitudinal Studies, *Pain Medicine*, 23(8), pp.1442–1456, https://doi.org/10.1093/pm/pnac029

[2] The Landmark Forum - Personal Development Courses – Landmark Worldwide

[3] Leyshon, C. and Hiddlestone-Mumford, J. (2023) Culture Based Performance: How CEOs and Leaders Can Co-Create High Performing Teams and Sustainable growth. CQify Publishing.

Epilogue

Overcoming Adversity and Becoming Resilient – The comforting relationship between Adversity and Resilience

by Dr Nii Amoo

As a numeracy and quantitative-minded person, I would love for my life to be a path of rationality and linearity and to be able to determine the future. But alas, in reality, it isn't so. Life is full of challenges, obstacles, and setbacks that often leave you feeling overwhelmed and defeated. However, there's good news in this because it is through these adversities that individuals' true strength and resilience shine. Think about the goldsmiths who continually try to refine their gold. Think about the pottery worker who moulds the clay until it turns into the finished object they desire. The comforting relationship is that resilience is what you can use to overcome adversity.

In this short piece, I want to use personal stories, psychological insights, and practical strategies to talk about life's journey of overcoming adversity and transforming oneself into a better position.

1. Acknowledging Adversity and Understanding Adversity:

It is very important to recognise life challenges, which may come in different forms of adversities and their impact on your life. This initial recognition of adversity should be the start and an opportunity to grow and transform your thinking and mindset.

2. Embracing Resilience and Cultivating an Inner Strength

It would help if you started developing resilience and the capacity to bounce back from adversity by identifying and using personal strengths and building a resilient mindset. Within the management literature (SWOT Analysis), this means using your internal strengths to overcome external threats. Try to also learn from resilient individuals and their strategies for coping.

3. Overcoming adversity

You can overcome adversities by reframing your perspectives and shifting the narrative about yourself and how you are perceived. So start by examining the power of perspective, reframing challenges positively, and changing your mindset to influence the perception and experience of adversity.

4. Building Emotional Resilience and Take Control

Our emotions or how we feel can immensely affect whatever we do. So start by managing your emotions when adversity is rearing its face. Developing an approach to first effectively managing stress, anxiety, and negative feelings – they are there and will, at some point in time, come along. But be prepared to take Control. Be the one in the driving seat. Be the pilot. Do this by developing emotional intelligence and self-awareness that cultivates self-compassion and practising self-care.

5. Turning Setbacks into Comebacks

Being in Control also means having the mindset to turn setbacks into positive outcomes by learning from your failures. Failures are there, so understanding the role of failures in personal growth and success is very important in your life's journey. So, develop a growth mindset by embracing failure as a stepping stone to the end product rather than a stop and throwing up your arms and giving up. Rather, leverage the failures as an opportunity for learning, adaptation, and improvement.

6. Becoming Stronger and Empowered

Look to develop a support network of family and friends by seeking help and guidance when needed – do not keep the problems to yourself alone. Look for trusted family and friends to share your problem – and who knows, it might not be a problem at all – just a worry thought. This is because the importance of social support in overcoming adversity cannot be overemphasised. So, build a strong network of friends, family, and mentors.

7. Setting Goals and Taking Action:

Harness your self-resilience by goal-setting and planning to overcome adversity. Create a roadmap for personal growth and transformation and take concrete and decisive steps towards achieving your desired outcomes.

8. Finding Meaning and Purpose:

Redefine your identity by discovering personal values, gaining a sense of purpose, and using adversity as a catalyst for personal transformation and sense-making.

Overcoming adversity is a journey that requires resilience, optimism, and self-reflection. By acknowledging our challenges, embracing our inner strength, and taking proactive steps towards personal growth, we can overcome adversity and emerge as stronger, wiser, and more empowered individuals. This chapter encourages readers to confront their adversities head-on, armed with the knowledge and tools necessary to transform their lives and create a future filled with resilience, purpose, and fulfillment.

About the Author

Dr Kieran Mervyn and Rohan Johnson are the co-authors of Overcoming and Becoming, the Art of Managing Change.

Dr Kieran Patrick Mervyn *is the CEO at Is Mise Cara Brain Disease Foundation and Co-Director at Finncara Consulting Ltd. He holds the position of Visiting Professor at London South Bank University. Additionally, he is an experienced research and management consultant in health and social care, specialising in evaluation and insight analysis. Dr Mervyn has contributed extensively to research projects focused on Leadership and Innovation. Notable organisations he has collaborated with include the Northern Leadership Academy (NLA), Centre for Innovation in Health Management (CIHM), and London South Bank University. His scholarly work has been published in prestigious international journals such as the Journal of the American Society for Information Science and Technology (JASIST), Information Communication and Society (ICS), and the International Journal of Leadership in Public Services (IJLPS).*

    Rohan Johnson *has worked for various organisations in the global high-tech industry in Ireland. With more than 20 years of experience, Rohan's areas of focus and expertise lie within the Information Technology and Partner Management consultancy field.*

    Prof Juanita Illingworth *was born to a man who went on to be Commissioner of Police elect and a lineage of hard-working achievers. Juanita is a woman who has lived a life full of extremes, which started by being born into a cult religion to a mother that had addiction and severe mental issues, the expected future looked* *bleak from a young age. It was the constant expectation of failure by teachers and society that prodded Juanita to want to prove them wrong by achieving as much as possible, against all odds. This drew in Juanita's interest in human behaviour and psychological impacts on performance both in and out of the workplace. Juanita attributes her personality and determination to succeed as resonating with her paternal character traits.*

What is success? For Juanita, it is to keep on developing as both a person and an academic. What is failure to Juanita? Being judged by others who deem what she has survived and endured as being impossible. Juanita teaches from the heart, in ensuring we have emotionally intelligent leaders in the future, where minds are open to realising how much it takes for someone 'non-traditional' to achieve within a 'traditional' environment.

Jonathan Buffard *is the director and founder of Bottom-Line Marketing Agency and a dynamic digital marketing leader with over 15 years of experience and an international background. He has lived in multiple countries, contributing to his adaptability and cultural awareness.*

Vjollca Behluli *an experienced development professional with a focus on democratic governance, project planning and development, and project management in Kosovo. She holds the position of Governance Advisor at GIZ, a Sustainable Municipal Services project in Kosovo, where she is dedicated to improving municipal services, particularly in waste management. Her extensive experience in these areas is evident through her work with esteemed international organizations such as USAID, the United Nations Mission in Kosovo, UNDP, HELVETAS Swiss Intercooperation, and GIZ. She holds an MSc in project management from the University of Roehampton in London, UK, and a master's in Local Governance and Democratic Society from the University of Gjilan in Kosovo.*

Benjamin Samuel *is of Nigerian descent, currently residing in Sabon Pegi Shabu, Lafia North Development Area, Nasarawa State, and is married with children. He advocates for appropriate data and information management/analysis, is a digital enthusiast, and believes in knowledge sharing and social inclusion to close the gap in digital inequalities. Benjamin holds an MSc in Information System Management and looks forward to a Ph.D. in Communication and Information Systems. He is also the board chairman of Doxa House Youth Empowerment and Inclusive De-*

velopment Initiative, a women, girls, and youth empowering/resilience-building initiative for marginalised and underserved communities.

Armando Licoze has over 25 years of leadership experience in Mozambique and South Africa international charities. He is the country director for Oasis in Mozambique, a global organisation focused on community transformation. Armando believes in the power of love and support in helping people address their concerns and grow. Apart from leading community projects, he researches health issues and publishes articles in reputable journals. Armando is also a Research Assistant at the University of Cape Town's Centre for Social Science Research. He holds a postgraduate degree in project management from the University of Roehampton Business School in London.

Ann Austin, a 25-year-old entrepreneur, founded Prazzle Magazine to empower creatives and challenge the notion that white-collar jobs are superior. With a BSc in Media and Communications and an MSc in marketing, Ann has over six years of experience as a digital marketing strategist, content developer, curator, and editor. Ann's vision includes building a digital ecosystem within the Prazzle app, enabling creatives to sell their works, receive support, and connect with like-minded individuals.

Gary Chandler a UK-born citizen migrated to Canada in 1973. In 1985, Gary joined the Royal Canadian Air Force, where he focused on training and flying heavy transport aircraft. After a decade of service in the Air Force, he transitioned to a civilian role in 1995. Gary joined Nav Canada as a project manager and the co-principal of an aviation change consulting company and later retired in 2000. Gary currently resides in Russell, Ontario, Canada, with his wife of 38 years. His journey from Portsmouth to Russell, from the Royal Canadian Air Force to his role in consultancy, tells a story of adaptation, growth, and enduring success.

Martin Imlach worked as a Lead Project Engineer in the oil and gas sector. He gradually progressed from being an LGV Mechanic to becoming the director of his own company, specializing in engineering and project management in various sectors such as construction, renewable energy, and oil and gas. As a leader, trainer, and mentor, Martin has led diverse and high-performing teams locally and internationally. Martin holds an MSc in engineering/industrial management from the University of Hull. He is an active STEM ambassador passionate about *knowledge sharing, particularly in the STEM fields.*

Carey-Ann Thurlow *is a dedicated professional with strong, extensive experience in the dental industry. As the CEO, President, and Co-founder of Risio Institute for Digital Dental Education, she leads a Canadian-wide Dental Assisting college. She actively participates in dental assisting boards at Canada's provincial and national levels. Her goal is consistently challenging and educating her team, encouraging them to think beyond the present and strive for greatness. In her free time, Carey-Ann enjoys mountain biking in the nearby mountains and supporting her sons on the football field. Her passion for learning and anticipation of the future remains unmatched.*

Angela Russell Grier *unveils the layers of an unimaginable life, providing an intimate glimpse into the raw, candid truth of survival, resilience, and the enduring spirit that defies even the harshest adversities. Orphaned and then adopted at the age of one, she assumed the role of caretaker for her adoptive parents by the age of ten. At fifteen, she discovered her mother lifeless on the kitchen floor, initiating the heartwrenching task of burying her mother, followed by her grandfather, father, and grandmother within seventeen months. Navigating the storm of grief with resilience beyond her years, Angela embarked on a solitary odyssey, self-raising in multiple countries from the age of fifteen. Moving through the decades, she married, divorced, and found her biological parents, only to bury them as well. She remarried, gave birth to their daughter, and finally felt she had the family she longed for, except tragedy revisited during this happiest time in her life. Her husband was struck with cancer and succumbed to the disease three years later. Angela works in the nonprofit sector, championing causes and supporting those in need. She just completed her MBA and is working on her MSc in Psychology to offer counselling support. By sharing her story, Angela aims to inspire others to grasp onto hope and reach the other side.*

Dr Angeliki Papasava *is an experienced academic and entrepreneur with over 15 years of teaching Management at various universities worldwide. She holds a PhD from the International School of Management and has started her own companies in Greece, Bulgaria, and the UK. Dr Papasava has also worked for multinational ICT companies, gaining valuable international experience. Currently, she is involved in postgraduate supervision, curriculum development, and partnership initiatives* with several universities, including the University of Hull Online, University of Portsmouth Online, University of Roehampton London Online, IMD Business School Lausanne, University of Sheffield, University of York, American Heritage College, and Edinburgh Napier University. Additionally, she serves as a PT Faculty Member at the American College of Greece and a Senior Lecturer at AthTech. Dr Papasava's research interests revolve around Entrepreneurship, Innovation, Human Resources Management, Leadership, and Strategy.

Julie Bagley was born in the UK and was a professional dancer who also sang and loved performing in theatre. She has lived in Germany and migrated to Australia in 1991. She is a mother of two adult daughters, is a two times divorcee, a widow, and now a life partner. She works part time, is an MBA student, a panellist, and a life-long scholar of personal growth and development. Julie has always had a passion for life and discovery. Surviving adversity has propelled her forwards to creating and living an amazing life.

Warren Dix a World-class Sales/Commercial Leader possessing an outstanding track record of scaling B2B technology firms across the UK, USA, and APAC, resulting in the closure of multiple long and complex B2B enterprise software and services deals. B2B SaaS in Procurement, Hospitality, Expense Management, and eCommerce.

You can connect with me on:

🌐 https://www.carabraindiseasefoundation.com
📘 https://www.facebook.com/FinncaraConsulting

Subscribe to my newsletter:

✉ https://www.carabraindiseasefoundation.com/news

Also by Dr Kieran Mervyn and Rohan Johnson

Is Mise Cara: Orbs, Souls and Holy Ghosts

Is Mise Cara: Orbs, Souls and Holy Ghosts is the story of Kieran's daughter Cara, a charming young girl who died of a brainstem tumour in December 2019.

Cara's death has opened a 'Pandora's Box' of paranormal and supernatural activity.

Proceeds from Kieran and wife Faye's publications:

- 'Is Mise Cara';

- 'Signs from Cara and Beyond' & this third book coauthored with Rohan Johnson

- 'Overcoming and Becoming: The Art of Managing Change' are donated to the Is Mise Cara Brain Disease Foundation.

www.carabraindiseasefoundation.com

E-book, hardback and audiobook versions of 'Overcoming and Becoming' are forthcoming.

Printed in Great Britain
by Amazon